TRU TWEETS

His social media phenomenon

Meryl Wages CIA Putin Hillary Rigged

James Poyner

Published by:
Wilkinson Publishing Pty Ltd
ACN 006 042 173
Level 4, 2 Collins Street
Melbourne, Vic 3000
Ph: 03 9654 5446
www.wilkinsonpublishing.com.au

Design Concepts by Matt Irwin Creative

Cover Design & Art Direction:
Matt Irwin

Illustrations and Layout:
Daniel Goodrich

The publisher's thanks go to journalists Ian and his wife the
late Patricia Huntley for their contribution to Trump Tweets
— the idea for the book and useful commentary from both
during its compilation.

Creator: Poyner, James, author.

Title: Trump Tweets: His social media phenomenon / James Poyner.

ISBN: 9781925265934 (paperback)

Subjects: Trump, Donald, 1946 | Trump, Donald, 1946, Political
and social views | Online social networks, Political aspects,
United States | Internet in political campaigns, United States
| Social media Political aspects, United States | Communication
in politics, Technological innovations, United States | Political
campaigns, United States, History, 21st century.

CONTENTS

About this book

Before he became the 45th President of the United States, Donald Trump was the head of the Trump conglomerate. His achievements as a businessman include:

- High-end real estate

- Trump branded hotels

- Trump branded golf courses

- Helped redevelop and co-owned the Wollman Ice Rink in Central Park

- Owned the Miss Universe beauty pageant until 2005

- Executive Producer and star of *The Apprentice* television series

His list of business achievements illustrates he is not just a successful businessman, he is also brand orientated.

We are living in the information age, an understanding of social media and (as we are a society of bloggers, tweeters, wall posters and Instagrammers; live-tweeting, hash-tagging and Periscoping every aspect of our lives) an awareness of brand has become essential if a person wants to cultivate a healthy digital presence, especially if that person is in a position of power and wants to engage with society-at-large.

Donald Trump's use of social media during his campaign for nomination and eventual election as President of the United States of America was unprecedented.

On November 13, 2016, Donald Trump appeared in his first television interview as President-elect. During the interview, Trump approximated that he had 28 million people following him across Facebook, Twitter and Instagram combined, he went on to say:

'I find it tremendous. It's a modern form of communication. There should be nothing we should be ashamed of... I think that social media has more power than the money they [Democrats] spent, and I think maybe to a certain extent, I proved that.'[1]

Trump's popularity on social media continues to grow. At the time this book went to print, on Twitter alone, Trump had 26.8 million followers. Donald Trump's Presidential account @POTUS had 16.2 million followers.

Trump's tenacious use of social media and apparent un-edited stream of consciousness approach to Twitter means whenever he posts anything on social media, it gets people talking. His presidential success was partly due to the way he harnessed social media platforms to engage with the everyman. This book is a Twitter-eye view of the 2016 US election and explores how Trump used social media as a campaign tool by examining the narrative of his tweets within the context of real-world events to not only show you Trump's most entertaining, bizarre and, on occasion, offensive social media activity but explore what it is that prompted him to say what he said. Through understanding Trump's approach to campaigning, we can gain insight into the way in which campaigns will be run and won by Western politicians in the decades to come and learn to recognise why seemingly outrageous responses on social media connect with people the way they do.

Politics is a constantly changing landscape, the information presented in this book was correct at the time of writing. Political appointments and policy decisions are accurate as of January 30, 2017.

---

1   CBS *60 Minutes* preview, November 13, 2016 – cbsnews.com

Prologue — Donald Trump vs the Republican Party

In 2009/10 unemployment in the US peaked at about 10%. By 2015, the number of unemployed, statistically, dropped, but unemployment levels were still higher than they were before the Global Financial Crisis, which meant it was easy to assume that the economic recovery, under President Barack Obama, had been unsuccessful.

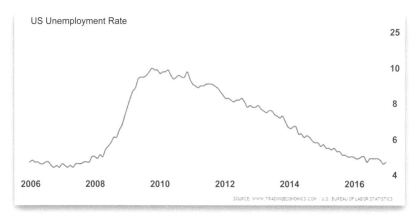

SOURCE: WWW.TRADINGECONOMICS.COM | U.S. BUREAU OF LABOR STATISTICS

On top of this, a Republican dominated Senate forced Obama to use executive orders and other Presidential powers to push through domestic policies that were otherwise blocked. The stage, as of June 2015, was a United States that had seen six years of high unemployment and a general feeling amongst many of dissatisfaction and disenfranchisement with the Obama-led government.

Trump entered stage right.

> *'Some of the candidates didn't know the air conditioner didn't work so they sweated like dogs. They didn't know the room was too big because they didn't have anybody there. How are they going to beat ISIS?'*
>
> *'We don't have victories anymore.'*

'Politicians are all talk, no action.'

'I watch the speeches of these people and they say the sun will rise, the moon will set all sorts of wonderful things will happen and people are saying what's going on, I just want a job.'

'Our county needs a truly great leader... we need a leader who can bring back our jobs... we need someone who can take the brand of the United States and make it great again... we need somebody who will take this country and literally make it great again.'

'Ladies and gentlemen I am officially running for President of the United States and we are going to make our country great again.'[2]

Campaign promises

'I would build a great wall, and nobody builds walls better than me, believe me, and I'll build them very inexpensively, I will build a great, great wall on our southern border. And I will have Mexico pay for that wall.'

'I would repeal and replace the big lie, ObamaCare.'

'Nobody would be tougher on ISIS than Donald Trump. Nobody.'[3]

Trump for President

In the beginning, there were 17 Republican candidates. Trump, a voracious businessman with no previous experience in public office was the obvious outsider, yet the polls put

---

2   Donald J. Trump's Presidential Announcement speech 6/6/15
      — YouTube Donald J. Trump for President official channel

3   Donald J. Trump 's Presidential Announcement speech 6/6/15
      — YouTube Donald J. Trump for President official channel

him at the centre of the fray, in the middle of the 10 most popular candidates. The moderators opened by questioning if any candidate would be unable to pledge their support for the eventual nominee and not run against them as an independent. After all, the point of the debates is to give each candidate a platform to express their intentions and to win favour with the registered members of the Republican Party who, ultimately, decide who runs against the Democrats.

Donald Trump raised his hand.

TRUMP: I can totally make that pledge. If I'm the nominee, I will pledge I will not run as an independent. But — and I am discussing it with everyone, but I'm, you know, talking about a lot of leverage. We want to win, and we will win. But I want to win as a Republican. I want to run as the Republican nominee.

Senator Rand Paul was visibly and audibly unimpressed with Trump's reasoning.

RAND: He's already hedging his bet on the Clintons, OK? So if he doesn't run as a Republican, maybe he supports Clinton, or maybe he runs as an Independent, but I'd say that he's already hedging his bets because he's used to buying politicians.

(Moderator) KELLY: Your Twitter account has several disparaging comments about women's looks. You once told a contestant on *Celebrity Apprentice* it would be a pretty picture to see her on her knees. Does that sound to you like the temperament of a man we should elect as president, and how will you answer the charge from Hillary Clinton, who is likely to be the Democratic nominee, that you are part of the war on women?

TRUMP: I think the big problem this country has is being politically correct.[4]

---

4   http://www.time.com/3988276/republican-debate-primetime-transcript-full-text

Trump's closing statement

'Our country is in serious trouble. We don't win anymore.

'We don't beat China in trade. We don't beat Japan, with their millions and millions of cars coming into this country, in trade. We can't beat Mexico, at the border or in trade.

'We can't do anything right. Our military has to be strengthened. Our vets have to be taken care of. We have to end ObamaCare, and we have to make our country great again, and I will do that.'[5]

Radioactive Trump

'I'm Donald Trump. I wrote *The Art of the Deal*. I say not in a braggadocious way, I've made billions and billions of dollars dealing with people all over the world, and I want to put whatever that talent is to work for this country so we have great trade deals.'

At the second debate, modest man Trump promised prosperity while cautious candidates carefully considered an atomic grade question.

TAPPER: You've dismissed him as an entertainer. Would you feel comfortable with Donald Trump's finger on the nuclear codes?

FIORINA: You know, I think Mr. Trump is a wonderful entertainer. He's been terrific at that business.

TAPPER: Governor Bush, would you feel comfortable with Donald Trump's finger on the nuclear codes?

BUSH: I think the voters will make that determination.[6]

---

5   http://www.time.com/3988276/republican-debate-primetime-transcript-full-text

6   http://www.time.com/4037239/second-republican-debate-transcript-cnn

A comic caper

HARWOOD: Mr Trump, you've done very well in this campaign so far by promising to build a wall and let another country pay for it, send 11 million people out of the country, cut taxes $US10 trillion without increasing the deficit, and make Americans better off because your greatness would replace the stupidity and incompetence of others. Let's be honest, is this a comic book version of a presidential campaign?

During the third debate, Trump tackled gun control issues; always a political talking point in the US. The National Rifle Association (NRA), who have long-standing ties with the Republican Party, and who had a reported five million members in late 2015, seem to use the second amendment as a banner. History would suggest that a pro-gun candidate would be popular with the Republican voters.

QUINTANILLA: Mr. Trump, you've said you have a special permit to carry a gun in New York.

TRUMP: Yes.

QUINTANILLA: After the Oregon mass shooting on October 1st, you said, 'By the way, it was a gun-free zone. If you had a couple of teachers with guns, you would have been a hell of a lot better off.'

TRUMP: Or somebody else. Right.

QUINTANILLA: Would you feel more comfortable if your employees brought guns to work?

TRUMP: I do carry on occasion, sometimes a lot. But I like to be unpredictable so that people don't know exactly.[7]

---

7   http://www.time.com/4091301/republican-debate-transcript-cnbc-boulder

And the winner is: Not appearing in this debate

Six months into the campaign for the Republican nomination Trump was still in the running. He chose not to attend the seventh debate.

KELLY: Let's address the elephant not in the room tonight.

(LAUGHTER)

Senator Cruz's response to the moderator's statement finishes with:

'Now that we've gotten the Donald Trump portion out of the way...'

Unable to get through the main campaign points without mentioning Donald Trump, collectively, the candidates referenced him a further 12 times.

CRUZ: I am glad Donald is running. I'm glad he has produced enormous enthusiasm, and, every Donald Trump voter or potential voter, I hope to earn your support.

RUBIO: Chris, let's begin by being clear what this campaign is about. It's not about Donald Trump. He's an entertaining guy. He's the greatest show on earth.

BUSH: I kind of miss Donald Trump. He was a little teddy bear to me.[8]

---

8   http://www.washingtonpost.com/news/the-fix/wp/2016/01/28/7th-republican-debate-transcript-annotated-who-said-what-and-what-it-meant/?utm_term=.eb644b83dd89

Trump — for the people

In the final Republican debate we witnessed Trump the politician; his rhetoric was noticeably calmer and more embracing.

'So I just say embrace these millions of people that now for the first time ever love the Republican Party. And unify. Be smart and unify.'[9]

The next day, Trump tweeted a 'thank you' message.

@realDonaldTrump 11 Mar 2016
Thank you America! #Trump2016 #MakeAmericaGreatAgain

The public's response was mostly positive.

@BornToBeGOP 11 Mar 2016
@realDonaldTrump **This was a great night for your campaign, we got to see President Trump.**

@dawnpsalm63 11 Mar 2016
@realDonaldTrump **great debate tonight. You gave clear direct answers. Your the only man brave enough to say there is a problem with Islam.**

@magicmetalninja 11 Mar 2016
@realDonaldTrump **Trump is America's fighter.** #PresidentTrump #AlwaysTrump

---

9   http://www.time.com/4255181/republican-debate-transcript-twelfth-cnn-miami

@09BRAININJURY 11 Mar 2016
@realDonaldTrump I want voters to know how good you've been to me always tweeted me back even before you were running for potus, your the best

@TrumpPenceUSA1 12 Mar 2016
@realDonaldTrump We LOVE YOU DONALD TRUMP!!!!!

The negative comments were, when compared to their usual calibre, average and were shot down swiftly by pro-Trump tweeters.

@LeeBangah 11 Mar 2016
@realDonaldTrump you not going to win

@secessionASAP 11 Mar 2016
@LeeBangah @realDonaldTrump yes he is

@kotacatchem 11 Mar 2016
@realDonaldTrump why do you always look so constipated?

@h_icks 11 Mar 2016
@kotacatchem @realDonaldTrump well he is full of shit so...

@GoatMouf 11 Mar 2016
@realDonaldTrump if your debate skills were a reality show you'd be fired, they are abysmal at best. Looked low energy and clueless tonight

@secessionASAP 11 Mar 2016
@GoatMouf @realDonaldTrump so says the goofy nerdy looking guy

@GoatMouf 11 Mar 2016
@secessionASAP @realDonaldTrump #HeLovesYou

Trump on the presidential campaign trail

July 2016: Trump is voted the nominee for the Republican Party

At the Republican National Convention, 2,472 delegates voted for their preferred candidate, Trump dominated.

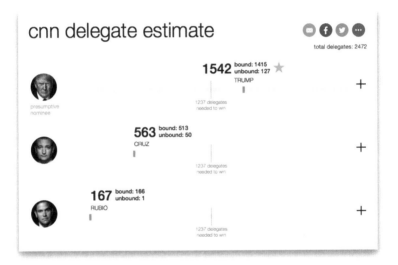

@realDonaldTrump 19 Jul 2016

Such a great honor to be the Republican Nominee for President of the United States. I will work hard and never let you down! AMERICA FIRST!

Reaction to Trump's nomination was the usual polar mix of love and hate.

@M_arcusC 20 Jul 2016
@realDonaldTrump you will never be President

@CAoutcast 20 Jul 2016
@M_arcusC @realDonaldTrump If he doesn't you
will totally lose your freedom..... Wimpy liberal man
voting for a woman? Sad!

@Rosechristenbe1 20 Jul 2016
@LMae1985 better than a lying, thief who should be
in jail. But facts elude you or u just don't care about
this country.

@LMae1985 20 Jul 2016
@Rosechristenbe1 I'm not didnt say I would vote for
hillary. Don't assume, it's ugly

@Cronikeys 20 Jul 2016
@realDonaldTrump God bless you and your whole
family! Love from Indiana

@TKMxEvolution 20 Jul 2016
@Cronikeys @realDonaldTrump pray to god you get
hit by a truck

@Cronikeys 20 Jul 2016
@TKMxEvolution @realDonaldTrump evil!

@TKMxEvolution 20 Jul 2016
@Cronikeys @realDonaldTrump rich coming from a
racist who supports a man who follows in the footsteps
of Hitler. Modern day nazi c**t.

@Zabusy 20 Jul 2016
@TKMxEvolution @Cronikeys @realDonaldTrump
I'm pretty sure if you don't vote trump there's a much
higher chance to get hit by a truck.

Trump vs the Democratic Party

Trump vs Hillary, Republicans vs Democrats. The real fight for the presidency began in late June. In an unprecedented and historic move, President Obama used his position to help Hillary curry favour with the public so they could secure the majority needed to win the November election.

In early July, President Obama flew Hilary Clinton and himself on Air Force One to a rally in North Carolina, where they appeared together. A number of news agencies covered the story:

'...a powerful symbol of the presidency that Obama appears happy to confer upon his preferred successor.' [10]

Trump used Twitter to ask...

@realDonaldTrump 4 Jul 2016
Why is President Obama allowed to use Air Force One on the campaign trail with Crooked Hillary? She is flying with him tomorrow. Who pays?

President Obama had already endorsed Hillary Clinton publicly, via a webcast in June, but he emphasised the importance of his endorsement at the Democratic National Convention when he said:

'There has never been a man or woman, not me, not Bill, nobody more qualified than Hillary to be president'. [11]

Long before Hillary Clinton was confirmed as the runner for the Democratic Party, the Republican Party viewed her as the candidate for the 2016 election, as this quote by Senator Rubio during the first Republican debate illustrates:

---

10   http://edition.cnn.com/2016/07/04/politics/obama-clinton-air-force-one-trump

11   http://www.bbc.com/news/election-us-2016-36911141

*'This election cannot be a resume competition.
It's important to be qualified, but if this election is
a resume competition, then Hillary Clinton's gonna
be the next president, because she's been in office
and in government longer than anybody else
running here tonight.'*

Trump beat 16 Republican rivals to secure the GOP
nomination, many of his Republican rivals were very
experienced Senators and, under normal circumstances,
would have been obvious presidential nominees.

> **@HillaryClinton** 22 Jul 2016
> **This is real—Donald Trump just accepted the
> @GOP nomination. RT if you agree: We can't let him
> become president.**

The tweet was retweeted 17,893 times.

After a hard battle within his own party, Trump had to face off
against a Democratic Party that were aiming for a third term,
trying to make history with the first female president, and who
were extremely determined to prevent Donald Trump from
becoming president.

> **@realDonaldTrump** 24 Jul 2016
> **Wow, President Obama's brother, Malik, just
> announced that he is voting for me. Was probably
> treated badly by president-like everybody else!**

> **@realDonaldTrump** 25 Jul 2016
> **Wow, the Republican Convention went so smoothly
> compared to the Dems total mess. But fear not, the
> dishonest media will find a good spinnnn**

@realDonaldTrump 26 Jul 2016
If Cory Booker is the future of the Democratic Party, they have no future! I know more about Cory than he knows about himself

@TheAnswererer 26 Jul 2016
@realDonaldTrump **Okay, thank you for making it clear that Cory got under your skin and you fear him you little man you.**

@DavidinTiburon 26 Jul 2016
@realDonaldTrump **Fortunately for you ... your votes are not educated. You know more about bankruptcy than anything else.**

@71Monk 26 Jul 2016
@realDonaldTrump **perhaps some time self reflecting would be wise, or are you afraid of what you will find.....emptiness**

@realDonaldTrump 31 Jul 2016
Nielson Media Research final numbers on ACCEPTANCE SPEECH: TRUMP 32.2 MILLION. CLINTON 27.8 MILLION. Thank you!

Count Crooked

Crooked Hillary: The nickname for Hillary Clinton used by Donald Trump, first used in April 2016.

Number of Crooked Hillary references in July: 72

Best Crooked tweets in July:

@realDonaldTrump 5 Jul 2016
Taxpayers are paying a fortune for the use of Air Force One on the campaign trail by President Obama and Crooked Hillary. A total disgrace!

@realDonaldTrump 6 Jul 2016
I have over seven million hits on social media re Crooked Hillary Clinton. Check it out Sleepy Eyes, @MarkHalperin @NBCPolitics

@realDonaldTrump 24 Jul 2016
Watched Crooked Hillary Clinton and Tim Kaine on 60 Minutes. No way they are going to fix America's problems. ISIS & all others laughing!

@realDonaldTrump 25 Jul 2016
Here we go again with another Clinton scandal, and e-mails yet (can you believe). Crooked Hillary knew the fix was in, B never had a chance!

Trump vs IS

Through the entire political process Trump consistently expressed disbelief at the government's handling of terrorist group Islamic State (IS) and campaigned he would take a more aggressive stance against them when he became Commander in Chief. Note that since the terrorist group was established in 1999 it has been through a number of rebrandings including ISIS (Islamic State of Iraq and Syria) and ISIL (Islamic State of Iraq and the Levant). In 2015, the military group officially changed its acronym to simply IS. For the purposes of context we will refer to them as IS, but for historical accuracy all quoted acronyms will not be altered.

'Islamic terrorism is eating up large portions of the Middle East,' Trump said during his candidacy speech. 'They've become rich. I'm in competition with them. They just built a hotel in Syria. Can you believe this? They built a hotel. When I have to build a hotel, I pay interest. They don't have to pay interest, because they took the oil that, when we left Iraq, I said we should've taken. Nobody would be tougher on ISIS than Donald Trump. Nobody.'

In December 2015, while the international community stepped up its involvement in the Syrian civil war, as a countermeasure to the threat posed by IS, Trump continued his anti-IS rhetoric during the second Republican debate:

> 'Syria's a mess. You look at what's going on with ISIS in there, now think of this: we're fighting ISIS. ISIS wants to fight Syria. Why are we fighting ISIS in Syria? Let them fight each other and pick up the remnants.'

@realDonaldTrump 27 Mar 2016
Another radical Islamic attack, this time in Pakistan, targeting Christian women & children. At least 67 dead, 400 injured. I alone can solve

@kianemadi 28 Mar 2016
@realDonaldTrump @CallumSkinner **I'm sure they would welcome his help with open arms**

@CallumSkinner 28 Mar 2016
@kianemadi **I'd happily let him go deep into Taliban territory alone..**

@kianemadi 28 Mar 2016
@CallumSkinner **I've heard they love receiving advice from Americans who openly call for the extinction of their religion**

In June 2016, in the midst of the political fray that was the fight for the nomination, an attack on a gay nightclub in Florida was credited to IS and reported by a number of news agencies to be the worst terror attack on US soil since September 11, 2001.

CNN

An American-born man who'd pledged allegiance to ISIS gunned down 49 people early Sunday at a gay nightclub in Orlando, the deadliest mass shooting in the United States and the nation's worst terror attack since 9/11, authorities said.[12]

SBS

BREAKING NEWS: Worst 'terror attack' since 9/11 in US history, 50 killed[13]

New York Times

At least 30 people inside were rescued, and even the hardened police veterans who took the building and combed through it, aiding the living and identifying the dead, were

---

12   http://edition.cnn.com/2016/06/12/us/orlando-nightclub-shooting

13   http://www.sbs.com.au/yourlanguage/hindi/en/article/2016/06/13/breaking-news-worst-terror-attack-911-us-history-50-killed

shaken by what they saw, said John Mina, the Orlando police chief. "Just to look into the eyes of our officers told the whole story," he said.

It was the worst act of terrorism on American soil since Sept. 11, 2001...[14]

Both Hillary and Trump reacted to the initial reports.

@HillaryClinton 12 Jun 2016
Woke up to hear the devastating news from FL. As we wait for more information, my thoughts are with those affected by this horrific act. -H

@realDonaldTrump 12 Jun 2016
Really bad shooting in Orlando. Police investigating possible terrorism. Many people dead and wounded.

Within a few hours of his initial tweet, Trump made a controversial decision to capitalise on the incident and bolster his view on the IS threat.

@realDonaldTrump 12 Jun 2016
Appreciate the congrats for being right on radical Islamic terrorism, I don't want congrats, I want toughness & vigilance. We must be smart!

With the media reporting that the gunman's family were originally from Afghanistan and may have immigrated to America during the 1979 Afghanistan/Soviet conflict, Trump used the opportunity to push his anti-immigration policy.[15]

14 https://www.nytimes.com/2016/06/13/us/orlando-nightclub-shooting.html?_r=0

15 https://www.washingtonpost.com/world/the-orlando-shooters-afghan-roots/2016/06/13/d89a8cd0-30e4-11e6-ab9d-1da2b0f24f93_story.html?utm_term=.10bef353cbf3

@realDonaldTrump 13 Jun 2016
In my speech on protecting America I spoke about a temporary ban, which includes suspending immigration from nations tied to Islamic terror.

Trump used the IS card on many of his policies. Even on topics such as selection for positions in government.

@realDonaldTrump 20 Oct 2016
I WILL DEFEAT ISIS. THEY HAVE BEEN AROUND TOO LONG! What has our leadership been doing? #DrainTheSwamp

@realDonaldTrump 5 Oct 2016
@mike_pence and I will defeat #ISIS. #VPDebate

@realDonaldTrump 23 Jul 2016
I highly recommend the just out book - THE FIELD OF FIGHT - by General Michael Flynn. How to defeat radical Islam.

General Flynn, a retired intelligence officer, who was appointed National Security advisor to the Trump administration, was reported to have extreme opinions about Islam, as this article from the *New York Times* indicated:

Michael Flynn, Anti-Islamist Ex-General, Offered Security Post, Trump Aide Says

President-elect Donald J. Trump has offered the post of national security adviser to Lt. Gen. Michael T. Flynn, potentially putting a retired intelligence officer who believes Islamist militancy poses an existential threat in one of the most powerful roles in shaping military and foreign policy, according to a top official on Mr. Trump's transition team.[16]

In February 2016, General Flynn tweeted a link to what looked like an IS training/PR video.

> @GenFlynn 27 Feb 2016
> **Fear of Muslims is RATIONAL: please forward this to others: the truth fears no questions...**

In August, *CNN* reported that Trump named President Obama as the 'founder of ISIS' and Hillary Clinton the MVP.

Host Hugh Hewitt asked Trump about the comments he made in Florida. Hewitt said he understood Trump to mean 'that he (Obama) created the vacuum, he lost the peace'.

Trump objected.

> *'No, I meant he's the founder of ISIS. I do. He was the most valuable player. I give him the most valuable player award. I give her, too, by the way, Hillary Clinton.'*
>
> *Hewitt pushed back, saying that Obama is 'not sympathetic' to IS and is in fact 'trying to kill them'.*
>
> *'I don't care', Trump said, according to a show transcript. 'He was the founder. The way he got out of Iraq was that, that was the founding of ISIS, okay?'[17]*

Hillary Clinton responded:

> @HillaryClinton 11 Aug 2016
> **No, Barack Obama is not the founder of ISIS.**

---

16 https://www.nytimes.com/2016/11/18/us/politics/michael-flynn-national-security-adviser-donald-trump.html?_r=0

17 http://edition.cnn.com/2016/08/11/politics/donald-trump-hugh-hewitt-obama-founder-isis

> **@HillaryClinton** 11 Aug 2016
> Anyone willing to sink so low, so often should never be allowed to serve as our Commander-in-Chief.

Trump later tweeted:

> **@realDonaldTrump** 12 Aug 2016
> Ratings challenged @CNN reports so seriously that I call President Obama (and Clinton) "the founder" of ISIS, & MVP. THEY DON'T GET SARCASM?

It is well reported that IS formed in war-torn Iraq and only became a global threat once the US-led coalition began to withdraw troops in 2014, but the conversation on Twitter chose to explore the definition of sarcasm, rather than the legitimacy of Trump's statement.

> **@jonrosenberg** 12 Aug 2016
> @realDonaldTrump **@CNN that's not sarcasm. You don't know how sarcasm works. You don't know what sarcasm means.**

> **@larryboensch** 14 Aug 2016
> @jonrosenberg @realDonaldTrump **@CNN That's right, sarcasm has nothing to do with tongue in cheek remarks about an incompetent leader.**

> **@jonrosenberg** 14 Aug 2016
> @larryboensch @realDonaldTrump **@CNN Please do humanity a favor and get a dictionary.**

> **@larryboensch** 14 Aug 2016
> @jonrosenberg @realDonaldTrump **@CNN Yes sir. One would think that a Websters New international would trump even the Ace of spades.**

@jonrosenberg 14 Aug 2016
@larryboensch @realDonaldTrump @CNN You
make about as much sense as Trump does. You
deserve him.

@larryboensch 14 Aug 2016
@jonrosenberg @realDonaldTrump @CNN That's
a small "t" seems you can write, but not read too well.
Try a 12 step program and a dictionary.

@jonrosenberg 14 Aug 2016
@larryboensch @realDonaldTrump @CNN
I understood the words you were using, you
patronizing hamsterf**ker. Bye now.

In November 2016, Trump first announced his intention
to 'consider' 'Mad Dog' Mattis for the role of Secretary
of Defense.

@realDonaldTrump 20 Nov 2016
General James "Mad Dog" Mattis, who is being
considered for Secretary of Defense, was very
impressive yesterday. A true General's General!

An article on the Business Insider website explained that
'Mad Dog' Mattis is known as a 'warrior monk' and earned his
nickname during the second battle of Fallujah. It also reported
that Mattis had described the action of shooting people as a
'hell of a hoot'.

'General Mattis is a strong, highly dignified man,' Trump told
the *New York Times* in late November. 'I met with him at
length and I asked him that question. I said, "What do you

think of waterboarding?" He said — I was surprised — he said, "I've never found it to be useful".' [18]

General James 'Mad Dog' Mattis is now officially serving as Secretary of Defense.

This fits nicely with Trump's philosophy on war and America's part in it. During his candidacy speech, Trump commented:

> *'I will find the General Patton or I will find General MacArthur, I will find the right guy, I will find the guy who will take the military and really make it work.'*

Trump's view of a military led by a Patton or MacArthur type could be considered nostalgic and possibly costly. War and the American war machine is very different to how it was in World War Two.

At the end of January 2017, the media reported on an incident in Yemen that was the result of direct action by troops on the ground.

A multitude of media outlets reported that a dawn raid in Yemen, which targeted Al-Qaeda fighters, resulted in 14 Al-Qaeda killed but 30 civilians too, which included 10 women and children.[19] During the same incident, US news sources reported that a member of the SEAL team that conducted the raid also died.[20]

---

18   http://www.businessinsider.com

19   http://www.independent.co.uk/news/world/middle-east/donald-trump-us-military-attack-yemen-civilians-women-children-dead-a7553121.html

20   https://www.nytimes.com/2017/01/29/world/middleeast/american-commando-killed-in-yemen-in-trumps-first-counterterror-operation.html?_r=0

Trump and Putin

Trump first imagined meeting Putin at the Miss Universe pageant in Moscow.

 @realDonaldTrump 19 Jun 2013
Do you think Putin will be going to The Miss Universe Pageant in November in Moscow — if so, will he become my new best friend?

 @realDonaldTrump 22 Mar 2014
Putin has become a big hero in Russia with an all time high popularity. Obama, on the other hand, has fallen to his lowest ever numbers. SAD

In December 2015, Trump made it onto President Putin's end-of-year honours list, which was widely reported in the media:

Reuters

Putin, speaking on Thursday at his year-end news conference, told reporters he welcomed Trump's desire for better relations with Russia.

"He is a very flamboyant man, very talented, no doubt about that. But it's not our business to judge his merits, it's up to the voters of the United States," Putin told reporters.

"He is an absolute leader of the presidential race, as we see it today. He says that he wants to move to another level relations, a deeper level of relations with Russia," Putin said. "How can we not welcome that? Of course, we welcome it."[21]

---

21   http://www.reuters.com/article/us-russia-putin-usa-trump-idUSKBN0U01NW20151217

Trump's focus on Russia during the election is about power and respect on the world stage, but in a Cold War domination sense of 'power'.

BBC News

Iran detains 10 US sailors after vessels stopped in the Gulf [22]

@realDonaldTrump 14 Jan 2016
Do you think Iran would have acted so tough if they were Russian sailors? Our country was humiliated.

@realDonaldTrump 14 May 2016
If Crooked Hillary Clinton can't close the deal on Crazy Bernie, how is she going to take on China, Russia, ISIS and all of the others?

@realDonaldTrump 27 Jul 2016
Funny how the failing @nytimes is pushing Dems narrative that Russia is working for me because Putin said "Trump is a genius." America 1st!

@realDonaldTrump 1 Aug 2016
When I said in an interview that Putin is "not going into Ukraine, you can mark it down," I am saying if I am President. Already in Crimea!

@realDonaldTrump 5 Sep 2016
President Obama & Putin fail to reach deal on Syria - so what else is new? Obama is not a natural deal maker. Only makes bad deals!

---

22 http://www.bbc.com/news/world-us-canada-35295766

During the election, claims that foreign (Russian) hackers were trying to influence the outcome of the election in a cyberattack were made public.

@realDonaldTrump 12 Dec 2016

Unless you catch "hackers" in the act, it is very hard to determine who was doing the hacking. Why wasn't this brought up before election?

@realDonaldTrump 15 Dec 2016

If Russia, or some other entity, was hacking, why did the White House wait so long to act? Why did they only complain after Hillary lost?

@realDonaldTrump 24 Dec 2016

Vladimir Putin said today about Hillary and Dems: "In my opinion, it is humiliating. One must be able to lose with dignity." So true!

@realDonaldTrump 30 Dec 2016

Russians are playing @CNN and @NBCNews for such fools - funny to watch, they don't have a clue! @FoxNews totally gets it!

One Twitter user responded to this statement by listing a number of articles appearing in the *Washington Post* and the *New York Times*:

Washington Post

U.S. government officially accuses Russia of hacking campaign to interfere with elections

The Obama administration on Friday officially accused Russia of attempting to interfere in the 2016 elections, including by hacking the computers of the Democratic National Committee and other political organizations.[23]

In a response to the cyberattack, President Obama took punitive action against Russia.

ABC News

Barack Obama orders expulsions of Russian diplomats, sanctions spies for interference in US election

Mr Obama had promised retaliation against Russia and it came in rolling announcements, with 35 Russian diplomats given 72 hours to leave the country.

Russia will also be blocked from accessing two compounds in New York and Maryland that were used by Russian personnel for "intelligence-related purposes".

In a further executive order, Mr Obama sanctioned two Russian intelligence agencies, the GRU and the FSB, four GRU officers and three companies "that provided material support to the GRU's cyber operations".[24]

Reuters

Putin earlier on Friday said he would not hit back for the U.S. expulsion of 35 suspected Russian spies by President Barack Obama, at least until Trump takes office on Jan 20.[25]

---

23 https://www.washingtonpost.com/world/national-security/us-government-officially-accuses-russia-of-hacking-campaign-to-influence-elections/2016/10/07/4e0b9654-8cbf-11e6-875e-2c1bfe943b66_story.html?utm_term=.20012d64d1c6

24 http://www.abc.net.au/news/2016-12-30/barack-obama-orders-expulsion-of-russian-officials/8153682

25 http://www.reuters.com/article/us-usa-russia-cyber-idUSKBN14I1TY

@realDonaldTrump 30 Dec 2016
Great move on delay (by V. Putin) — I always knew he was very smart!

In January 2017, a British newspaper published a story regarding an intelligence briefing that Donald Trump received. It was reported the briefing contained details of Russian cyberattack during the election campaign:

The Independent

The president-elect has refused to agree with President Barack Obama and domestic intelligence agencies that Russia hacked the US's cyber systems in order to boost his candidacy and propel him into the White House, at the expense of his rival Hillary Clinton.

"While Russia, China, other countries, outside groups and people are consistently trying to break through the cyber infrastructure of our governmental institutions, businesses and organisations including the Democratic National Committee, there was absolutely no effect on the outcome of the election, including the fact that there was no tampering whatsoever with voting machines," he said.

The briefing with Mr Trump comes the same day that a classified report given to President Obama this week is expected to be made public and to shed light on the evidence gathered by US intelligence agencies that led them to believe that Russia was behind the attack. Evidence includes phone calls from Russian officials, congratulating Mr Trump on his win. Mr Trump questioned why NBC gained first access to the report, labelling it "politics".[26]

---

26   http://www.independent.co.uk/news/world/americas/donald-trump-russia-cyber-hack-vladimir-putin-president-barack-obama-fbi-cia-intelligence-briefing-a7513966.html

In the wake of the Russian hacking allegations Trump went on the offensive, he accused news agencies and other politicians of conspiracy and 'fake news' and repeatedly he had no links with Russia.

@realDonaldTrump 6 Jan 2017
How did NBC get "an exclusive look into the top secret report he (Obama) was presented?" Who gave them this report and why? Politics!

@realDonaldTrump 11 Jan 2017
Russia just said the unverified report paid for by political opponents is "A COMPLETE AND TOTAL FABRICATION, UTTER NONSENSE." Very unfair!

@realDonaldTrump 11 Jan 2017
Russia has never tried to use leverage over me. I HAVE NOTHING TO DO WITH RUSSIA — NO DEALS, NO LOANS, NO NOTHING!

@realDonaldTrump 13 Jan 2017
Totally made up facts by sleazebag political operatives, both Democrats and Republicans - FAKE NEWS! Russia says nothing exists. Probably...

@realDonaldTrump 16 Jan 2017
@FoxNews "Outgoing CIA Chief, John Brennan, blasts Pres-Elect Trump on Russia threat. Does not fully understand." Oh really, couldn't do...

@realDonaldTrump 16 Jan 2017
much worse - just look at Syria (red line), Crimea, Ukraine and the build-up of Russian nukes. Not good! Was this the leaker of Fake News?

August: Fly in the ointment

Facebook
August 3, 2016
Donald J. Trump

STATEMENT IN RESPONSE TO PRESIDENT OBAMA'S FAILED LEADERSHIP

Obama-Clinton have single-handedly destabilized the Middle East, handed Iraq, Libya and Syria to ISIS, and allowed our personnel to be slaughtered at Benghazi. Then they put Iran on the path to nuclear weapons. Then they allowed dozens of veterans to die waiting for medical care that never came.

Hillary Clinton put the whole country at risk with her illegal email server, deleted evidence of her crime, and lied repeatedly about her conduct which endangered us all. They released criminal aliens into our country who killed one innocent American after another -- like Sarah Root and Kate Steinle -- and have repeatedly admitted migrants later implicated in terrorism. They have produced the worst recovery since the Great Depression. They have shipped millions of our best jobs overseas to appease their global special interests. They have betrayed our security and our workers, and Hillary Clinton has proven herself unfit to serve in any government office.

She is reckless with her emails, reckless with regime change, and reckless with American lives. Our nation has been humiliated abroad and compromised by radical Islam brought onto our shores. We need change now.

- Donald J. Trump[27]

---

27   https://www.facebook.com/DonaldTrump/posts/10157423383850725

Trump entered his first full month as the Republican nominee. He started by accusing a fire marshal of 'turning away supporters' at a rally due to 'political motivations'.

This story had a number of angles. ABC News Politics posted a clip on Twitter of Trump issuing a statement to the press at the event:

@ABCPolitics 2 Aug 2016
@realDonaldTrump **tells press that rally crowd in Columbus, OH was limited "for political reasons."**

Trump said:

> *'I just want to tell you, we've had thousands of people outside, thousands. They were turned away by...*
> *for political reasons, purely for political reasons.'*

Trump chose not to criticise or confront the fire marshal through social media, instead he retweeted a story written by thegatewaypundit.com — a politics blog with centre-right overtones.

@gatewaypundit **Retweeted by** @realDonaldTrump
1 Aug 2016 **Democrat Fire Marshal Turns THOUSANDS of Trump Supporters Away at Columbus Rally**
shar.es/1Z4sbo **via** @gatewaypundit

Aside from this, the incident received minimal press coverage. The next day, *Politico* magazine covered the story in more detail:

Politico

His own senior campaign staff officials were fully aware and had agreed in writing that the Trump event in Columbus was to be restricted to a maximum of 1,000 people, according to documents signed on Friday, July 29, between the Trump campaign and Columbus Convention Center for the Monday event, and obtained by Politico.[28]

Meanwhile, Trump moved onto generating support in the mining and manufacturing intensive states of Pennsylvania and West Virginia (WV).

@realDonaldTrump 2 Aug 2016
Vast numbers of manufacturing jobs in Pennsylvania have moved to Mexico and other countries. That will end when I win!

@MooneyforWV 8 Aug 2016
The WV economy is hurting under Obama-Clinton, @realDonaldTrump will bring real prosperity for all! #trumpindetroit #TrumpPence16 #wvpol

(Alex Mooney (@MooneyforWV) is the Conservative congressman for West Virginia.)

@realDonaldTrump 10 Aug 2016
Great meeting w/ coal miners & leaders from the Virginia coal industry- thank you! #MAGA

In August, Trump unveiled his economic policy during a rally in Detroit. He stated he would cut taxes and eliminate regulations 'which are not necessary, do not improve public safety, and which needlessly kill jobs'.[29]

The part of Trump's economic policy that appealed to most voters was his pledge to create 25 million jobs over the next decade. He vowed to make this happen by incentivising

---

28   http://www.politico.com/magazine/story/2016/08/donald-trump-2016-rally-size-214132

29   http://fortune.com/2016/08/08/trump-economic-speech-detroit

businesses to return to the US as well as providing tax relief to small businesses and low-wage families. His plan is best summarised in this tweet from April 2015:

> @realDonaldTrump 28 Apr 2015
> **The best social program, by far, is a JOB! Our jobs are being taken away from us by China and many other countries - incompetent leader.**

In August 2016, Hillary Clinton reacted to his economic plan:

> **@HillaryClinton** 8 Aug 2016
> **Donald Trump's economic plan:**
> **1. Lower wages**
> **2. Fewer jobs**
> **3. More debt**
> **4. Tax breaks for the 0.1%**

The title card match: Trump vs Obama

> @realDonaldTrump 2 Aug 2016
> **President Obama will go down as perhaps the worst president in the history of the United States!**

Modern politics has a very strong partisan vein running through it, but the battle between the Democrats and Republicans became very personal in August when Trump and Obama publicly denounced each other's intentions and abilities.

The core of this fight was Trump's stance on Islam. In the months leading up to Trump's 'Statement on Preventing Muslim immigration', issued on December 7, 2015, there were a number of attacks around the world, some which were accredited to Islamic State (IS).

To understand the Trump/Obama media war in early August 2016, we need to explore the increasing global threat of IS and the evolution of Trump's stance on the terror group.

November 13, 2015 — Paris

ABC News

More than 120 people have been killed in a series of coordinated terrorist attacks across Paris, including a massacre at a rock concert.

Gunmen and bombers also attacked busy restaurants and bars, and explosions were heard near a stadium in what a shaken French president Francois Hollande described as an unprecedented terrorist attack.

More than 350 people were injured in the attacks, about 100 of those seriously.[30]

Islamic State claimed responsibility for the attack.

December 2, 2015 — San Bernardino

New York Times

F.B.I. Treating San Bernardino Attack as Terrorism Case

On the day she and her husband killed 14 people and wounded 21 others in San Bernardino, Calif., a woman pledged allegiance to the Islamic State in a Facebook post, officials said Friday, as the F.B.I. announced that it was treating the massacre as an act of terrorism.

"The investigation so far has developed indications of radicalization by the killers, and of potential inspiration by foreign terrorist organizations," the F.B.I. director, James B. Comey, said at a news conference here. But he said that

---

30   http://www.abc.net.au/news/2015-11-14/paris-attacks-120-dead-in-shootings-explosions/6940722

investigators had not found evidence that the killers were part of a larger group or terrorist cell. The couple died in a shootout with the police on Wednesday."

The Islamic State said in an online radio broadcast on Saturday that two of its followers had carried out the attack, Reuters reported. "Two followers of Islamic State attacked several days ago a center in San Bernardino in California," said the statement, issued on the group's daily broadcast al-Bayan.[31]

@realDonaldTrump 2 Dec 2015
#TeamTrump. **Police and law enforcement seem to have killed one of the California shooters and are in a shootout with the others. Go police**

December 7, 2015

DonaldJTrump.com

Donald J. Trump Statement on Preventing Muslim Immigration

Donald J. Trump is calling for a total and complete shutdown of Muslims entering the United States until our country's representatives can figure out what is going on.

Mr. Trump stated, "Without looking at the various polling data, it is obvious to anybody the hatred is beyond comprehension. Where this hatred comes from and why we will have to determine. Until we are able to determine and understand this problem and the dangerous threat it poses, our country cannot be the victims of horrendous attacks by people that believe only in Jihad, and have no sense of reason or respect for human life."[32]

---

31   https://www.nytimes.com/2015/12/05/us/tashfeen-malik-islamic-state.html?_r=0

32   https://www.donaldjtrump.com/press-releases/donald-j.-trump-statement-on-preventing-muslim-immigration

Trump continued his 'anti-Muslim' sentiment and stated the UK had a Muslim problem.

> **@realDonaldTrump** 10 Dec 2015
> **The United Kingdom is trying hard to disguise their massive Muslim problem. Everybody is wise to what is happening, very sad! Be honest.**

Trump's statement can be interpreted as the dictionary definition of racism.

> *Racism: The belief that all members of each race possess characteristics, abilities, or qualities specific to that race, especially so as to distinguish it as inferior or superior to another race or races.* [33]

Trump needed to find a way to explode the issue, to make his actions appear defensive. Twitter users in the UK did not take kindly to Trump's tweet.

> @imbadatlife 10 Dec 2015
> @realDonaldTrump I agree. I live on the 4th floor and he's so massive he keeps looking in my window as he walks past. Lovely bloke though.

> @imbadatlife 10 Dec 2015
> @realDonaldTrump So few people know that Big Ben is actually an extremely tall Muslim in disguise. Only job he could get. Been years now.

> @omerwahaj 10 Dec 2015
> @imbadatlife @realDonaldTrump Big Ben Laden

---

33   https://en.oxforddictionaries.com/definition/racism

Trump continued by praising an article by *Daily Mail* columnist and *The Apprentice* (UK) Season 3 contestant, Katie Hopkins.

@realDonaldTrump 10 Dec 2015

Thank you to respected columnist Katie Hopkins of DailyMail.com for her powerful writing on the U.K.'s Muslim problems.

Daily Mail

KATIE HOPKINS: Don't demonise Trump, he speaks for millions of Americans. And who can blame them for not wanting to end up like us?[34]

Her column defended Trump by rationalising that it would be logistically impossible for a Trump administration to enact a Muslim ban. She also criticised a petition to 'Ban Donald Trump from the UK'.

Her column does provide some insight into his success and even draws parallels between her own denouncement by the UK public.

'I hear cries that he is a blithering idiot. I have often been called a deranged fool. But if this were true you could ignore me, ignore us, imaging the two of us shouting naked at the rain.' [35]

In 2013, Katie Hopkins offended the British public by saying that ginger babies are harder to love, that she wouldn't hire fat people, or let her children play with youngsters named Chardonnay or Tyler. She said, 'If I am the most hated

---

34   http://www.dailymail.co.uk/news/article-3353060/Calm-Trump-s-Muslim-travel-ban-never-going-happen-isn-t-America-just-little-bit-lucky-suggest-it.html

35   As above

*woman in Britain, we've all lost a bit of perspective.
I'm just telling the truth.'* [36]

Yet Trump did not need to rely on media bedfellows with
a history of hatred to draw a reaction out of people.

@realDonaldTrump 10 Dec 2015
**In Britain, more Muslims join ISIS than join the
British army.**

Trump referenced conservative American magazine
nationalreview.com as his source.

March 22, 2016 — Brussels

Five months after Paris, another European city came under
terrorist attack.

BBC News — A timeline of events

Bombings at Brussels airport and a metro station in the
city on Tuesday 22 March killed 32 people from around
the world.

Many more were injured in the attacks. The toll does not
include three bombers who died.

Twin blasts struck the main terminal of Zaventem
international airport, in the north-east of the city.

Another explosion hit the Maelbeek metro station in the
city centre, close to several European Union institutions.

Who carried out the attacks?

The so-called Islamic State group said it was behind
the attacks.[37]

---

36   http://www.dailymail.co.uk/femail/article-2361674/Katie-Hopkins-If-I-hated-
     woman-Britain-weve-lost-bit-perspective-Im-just-telling-truth.html

37   http://www.bbc.com/news/world-europe-35869985

@realDonaldTrump 22 Mar 2016
Incompetent Hillary, despite the horrible attack in Brussels today, wants borders to be weak and open- and let the Muslims flow in. No way!

The Independent

Up to 5,000 jihadists are feared to be in Europe after returning from terrorist training camps, the head of Europol has said.

Rob Wainwright, director of the EU-wide law enforcement agency, predicted further attacks by Isis following the massacres in Paris that killed 130 people in November.[38]

@realDonaldTrump 24 Mar 2016
Just announced that as many as 5000 ISIS fighters have infiltrated Europe. Also, many in U.S. I TOLD YOU SO! I alone can fix this problem!

This tweet is in reference to a comment he made in an interview with journalist Maria Bartiromo.

New York Times
January 2016

Asked by the Fox Business Network anchor Maria Bartiromo about the feasibility of his proposal to bar foreign Muslims from entering the United States, Mr. Trump argued that Belgium and France had been blighted by the failure of Muslims in these countries to integrate.

---

38   http://www.independent.co.uk/news/world/europe/isis-up-to-5000-jihadists-in-europe-after-returning-from-terror-training-camps-daesh-islamic-state-a6885961.html

"There is something going on, Maria," he said. "Go to Brussels. Go to Paris. Go to different places. There is something going on and it's not good, where they want Sharia law, where they want this, where they want things that — you know, there has to be some assimilation. There is no assimilation. There is something bad going on."[39]

@realDonaldTrump 23 Jun 2016
**ISIS threatens us today because of the decisions Hillary Clinton has made along with President Obama."
— Donald J. Trump**

In late July/early August 2016, Trump's continual bashing of Hillary Clinton, President Obama and the Democratic Party, and using the media hype surrounding Islamic State as a tool to justify his controversial Muslim immigration plan came to a head.

BBC News

Fury as Trump mocks Muslim soldier's mother Ghazala Khan

Republican presidential hopeful Donald Trump has attracted outrage by mocking a dead US Muslim soldier's mother.

Ghazala Khan stood silently next to her husband as he attacked Mr Trump in an emotional speech to the Democratic National Convention on Thursday.

Mr Trump suggested she may not have been allowed to speak.

---

39   https://www.nytimes.com/2016/01/28/world/europe/trump-finds-new-city-to-insult-brussels.html

Republicans and Democrats said the Republican candidate's comments were no way to talk of a hero's mother. Mrs Khan said she was upset by his remarks.[40]

@realDonaldTrump 31 Jul 2016
I was viciously attacked by Mr. Khan at the Democratic Convention. Am I not allowed to respond? Hillary voted for the Iraq war, not me!

The response on Twitter to Trump's statement accurately depicted the divide that his anti-Muslim stance created.

@nouripour 31 Jul 2016
@realDonaldTrump He did not attack you for the Iraq war, but for your campaign of rhetorical segregation. You don't care for details, right?

@DSF2020 31 Jul 2016
@nouripour @realDonaldTrump We don't need to segregate them, all we need to do is DO NOT accept them. We don't want them in our country.

Trump asserted the point that his comments were about the greater threat.

@realDonaldTrump 1 Aug 2016
This story is not about Mr. Khan, who is all over the place doing interviews, but rather RADICAL ISLAMIC TERRORISM and the U.S. Get smart!

Trump's statements about Mr Khan clearly infuriated President Obama who, in front of the Prime Minister of Singapore, declared that Trump was unfit for the job:

---

40   http://www.bbc.com/news/election-us-2016-36935175

CNN

Obama says Trump 'unfit' for presidency

President Barack Obama offered one of his sharpest denunciations of Donald Trump to date Tuesday, declaring the Republican nominee entirely unfit to serve as president and lambasting Republicans for sticking by their nominee.

The strong rebuke in the White House East Room came after Trump's criticism of the family of a slain Muslim US soldier, along with comments that displayed apparent confusion related to the Russian incursion into Ukraine.

"The Republican nominee is unfit to serve as president," Obama said at a White House news conference with the Prime Minister of Singapore. "He keeps on proving it."[41]

Donald Trump went on the offensive, specifically targeting Obama.

@realDonaldTrump 2 Aug 2016
President Obama will go down as perhaps the worst president in the history of the United States!

@realDonaldTrump 5 Aug 2016
Obama's disastrous judgment gave us ISIS, rise of Iran, and the worst economic numbers since the Great Depression!

Throughout the rest of Trump's campaign, Trump and Obama never saw eye-to-eye. Trump regularly took pot-shots at Obama and his policies throughout the latter half of 2016 and early into 2017. President Obama swung his final punch days before Trump's inauguration, during his last press conference

---

41 http://edition.cnn.com/2016/08/02/politics/obama-says-trump-unfit-for-presidency

with the mainstream media as President. Obama emphasised the importance of a 'free press' and their function to keep government honest,[42] which felt like a final counter to Trump's persistent accusations of a dishonest and biased mainstream media that spreads fake news.

Given the ferocity in which Trump attacked the *New York Times* during the campaign and the noticeable drop in his social media presence immediately after inauguration, it felt like maybe Trump did just use an aggressive stance against a news agency who were anti-him. But on January 29, 2017 Trump reignited his criticism of the mainstream media.

@realDonaldTrump 29 Jan 2017
Somebody with aptitude and conviction should buy the FAKE NEWS and failing @nytimes and either run it correctly or let it fold with dignity!

---

42   http://www.usatoday.com/story/news/politics/2017/01/18/watch-live-president-obama-holds-final-press-conference/96720584

Trump vs ObamaCare

US Healthcare before the Patient Protection and Affordable Care Act (ObamaCare)

The US healthcare system is largely made up of privately funded hospitals that require the patient to pay for their healthcare. As this can be extremely expensive, health insurance is, essentially, mandatory for anyone who wants access to hospital treatment in the US.

This is not to say that if someone cannot afford health insurance they are ostracised from the health system. Veterans, the elderly, young people with special needs, and those with end-stage renal disease, for example, are entitled to Medicare, a social insurance program.

Low income families are eligible to apply for Medicaid a social welfare system which provides those eligible with access to general medical and hospital services.

ACA's death by 1000 cuts via the Trump social media machine

One of President Obama's legacy goals was the establishment of the Affordable Care Act (ACA). Before it was enacted in 2010, the number of US citizens without healthcare insurance reached 48.6 million.

Statistics indicate that the ACA may have been working, at least in the context of increasing the number of Americans who have health insurance. Over five years (2010 – 2015) the number of Americans with a form of health insurance increased by 20 million. In the past Trump also said, on record, that he recognised there is a health-gap in the US between people with access to health insurance and those without. This was brought up during the first Republican debate.

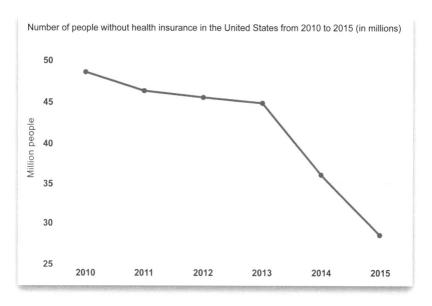

Number of people without health insurance in the United States from 2010 to 2015 (in millions)

'It could have worked in a different age...what I'd like to see is a private system without the artificial lines around every state... get rid of the artificial lines and then we will have great plans... then we have to take care of the people who cannot take care of themselves and I will do that through a different system.'[43]

At the beginning of the 21st century, Trump was in favour of social healthcare.[44] However since 2011, since the seed of presidency began to germinate, Trump became aggressively anti-ACA/ObamaCare.

43   http://www.time.com/3988276/republican-debate-primetime-transcript-full-text

44   http://www.businessinsider.com.au/trump-supports-national-health-care-2011-4?r=US&IR=T

@realDonaldTrump 8 Feb 2012
ObamaCare is an attack on our country's identity. The latest victim is the Catholic church. It must be full repealed. @BarackObama

As if laying the foundations for a total reversal of the ACA, throughout its relatively short lifespan Trump found flaws that fit nicely with his campaign policies, such as boosting the economy by encouraging small businesses to flourish.

@realDonaldTrump 16 Feb 2012
Gallup poll proves that @BarackObama's regulation and Obamacare are stopping small business owners from hiring SHOCK!

Gallup

Health Costs, Gov't Regulations Curb Small Business Hiring

Nearly half of small-business owners name these issues

PRINCETON, NJ -- U.S. small-business owners who aren't hiring -- 85% of those surveyed -- are most likely to say the reasons they are not doing so include not needing additional employees; worries about weak business conditions, including revenues; cash flow; and the overall U.S. economy. Additionally, nearly half of small-business owners point to potential healthcare costs (48%) and government regulations (46%) as reasons. One in four are not hiring because they worry they may not be in business in 12 months.[45]

---

45   http://www.gallup.com/poll/152654/Health-Costs-Gov-Regulations-Curb-Small-Business-Hiring.aspx

@realDonaldTrump 21 Mar 2013
Make no mistake, Obamacare is the first step towards changing our health system into single payer. Just a disaster.

As proof that any media event is good fodder for pressing an opinion and possessing no qualms about capitalising on an act of terrorism to push the anti-ObamaCare rhetoric, Trump attacked the aspect of the ACA which focuses on increasing the societal availability of medical insurance by linking it to the medical treatment the Boston marathon bomber received once he had been captured.

The Telegraph

Boston bomber arrested: how David Henneberry found Dzhokhar Tsarnaev in his garden

In an official photograph released by authorities, Dzhokhar is seen captured on the ground, surrounded by police, and receiving first aid. His shirt is pulled up revealing wounds to his neck. He was also shot in the leg.[46]

@realDonaldTrump 20 Apr 2013
Get ALL the info, then quick trial, then death penalty for the Boston killer of innocent children and people! Do not be kind.

@realDonaldTrump 20 Apr 2013
Is the Boston killer eligible for Obama Care to bring him back to health?

---

46   http://www.telegraph.co.uk/news/worldnews/northamerica/usa/10007969/
      Boston-bomber-arrested-how-David-Henneberry-found-Dzhokhar-Tsarnaev-in-
      his-garden.html

@realDonaldTrump 24 Apr 2013
The Boston killer applying today for ObamaCare.
He demands that medical bills be taken care of
immediately. Does this include dental?

On what seemed like monthly regularity, Trump slowly added
to his rhetoric with a series of glancing blows.

@realDonaldTrump 27 Sep 2013
Spanish version of ObamaCare website delayed.
Hitting google translate apparently too complicated.
#MakeDCListen

@realDonaldTrump 28 Oct 2013
Thanks to ObamaCare's device tax, Boston Scientific
plans to cut 1,500 jobs. ObamaCare will kill ingenuity.

@realDonaldTrump 14 Nov 2013
Breaking news--negotiations with Iranians broke down
because Obama insisted that they use ObamaCare.

@realDonaldTrump 18 Apr 2014
CBO now estimates that over 2.5M will lose jobs
directly because of ObamaCare. REPEAL now before
it is too late.

The news stories generated by the report from the
Congressional Budget Office (CBO) were looked into by
Website factcheck.org. The site analyses the factual accuracy
of statements made by politicians in the US. It categorised this
story as 'Party Lines', meaning it was spun by the Republicans
to show a negative impact on jobs.

@realDonaldTrump 16 Sep 2014
In order to stop the Ebola outbreak in Africa, perhaps the President should put all Africans on ObamaCare rather than sending the troops!

@realDonaldTrump 9 Feb 2016
We will immediately repeal and replace ObamaCare - and nobody can do that like me. We will save $'s and have much better healthcare!

In the first half of January 2017, with his inauguration less than a month away, Trump pushed his anti-ACA agenda and used the recent rise in the cost of premiums as ammunition.

@realDonaldTrump 3 Jan 2017
The Democrat Governor of Minnesota said "The Affordable Care Act (ObamaCare) is no longer affordable!" - And, it is lousy healthcare.

@realDonaldTrump 4 Jan 2017
Republicans must be careful in that the Dems own the failed ObamaCare disaster, with its poor coverage and massive premium increases......

@realDonaldTrump 4 Jan 2017
massive increases of ObamaCare will take place this year and Dems are to blame for the mess. It will fall of its own weight - be careful!

@realDonaldTrump 13 Jan 2017
The "Unaffordable" Care Act will soon be history!

The response from Twitter came from writers and media broadcasting professionals.

@DanHowdle
@realDonaldTrump ... he said as he bit the head off
another child.

@DavidGMcAfee
I'm sorry, @realDonaldTrump, but until there's is a
replacement, I don't know what you're so happy about.

@matthaig1
@realDonaldTrump Make American Graves Again!

What ACA did was grant millions of Americans access to
healthcare by modifying the existing system. If President
Trump does repeal the ACA, the big question is, what will
he replace it with? During the first Republican debate, when
the Republican party had 17 candidates that needed to be
trimmed, back when Trump was still considered 'not a serious
threat' he was questioned about his alternative plan to
the ACA.

> 'What I'd like to see is a private system without the
> artificial lines around every state. I have a big company
> with thousands of employees. And if I'm negotiating in BY
> or NJ or CA, I have like one bidder. Nobody can bid. You
> know why? Because the insurance companies are making
> a fortune because they have control of the politicians.
> They're making a fortune. Get rid of the artificial lines and
> you will have yourself great plans. And then we have to
> take care of the people that can't take care of themselves.
> And I will do that through a different system.'[47]

What Obama did with the ACA was to modify the old US
healthcare system by expanding the reach of the Medicare
and Medicaid federal programs as well as introduce penalties

---

47   http://www.time.com/3988276/republican-debate-primetime-transcript-full-text

to businesses of a certain size who did not supply health insurance to their employees.

What Trump appears to be proposing is to go back to the old system, but make health insurance a national level policy, instead of a state level policy, which would mean that businesses who operate in multiple states would only need one employee insurance policy. Trump has also suggested that the entire healthcare system be based on the mechanics of a free-market-economy, this should mean that price reflects demand and is not subject to interference from government or big businesses. But as the medical system is pretty much split between government and big business, how Trump's system would work is unclear.

Trump has also failed to address the problem of "people who can't take care of themselves".[48]

January 2017

Within hours of his inauguration President Trump signed his first executive order: 'Minimising the economic burden of the Patient Protection and Affordable Care Act pending repeal'.

The order allowed all departments of government, relevant to the ACA, to relax, make exceptions and even ignore aspects of the ACA to help the public ease into a new, yet currently undefined and unimplemented system.

In many ways, Trump lived up to his promise to immediately repeal the ACA. However, this executive order could cause more problems than it intended to solve. On January 23, thehill.com reported on a plan by two Republican senators to help bring the Democrats on board by giving states the option to use the ACA or a proposed Patient Freedom Act (PFA):

---

48   http://www.time.com/3988276/republican-debate-primetime-transcript-full-text

The Hill

Under the plan, known as the Patient Freedom Act, state legislatures would have the choice of whether to keep ObamaCare operating in their states, complete with its subsidies, mandates and protections for people with pre-existing conditions.

Other states, the senators say, could opt into an alternative plan that would provide a uniform tax credit linked to a health savings account to help people afford a basic, less comprehensive health insurance plan.[49]

The article reported that this proposal had already been rejected, but with the Trump executive order in place, Senators will be desperate to find an alternative system to implement.

---

49   http://thehill.com/policy/healthcare/315670-gop-senators-give-states-the-option-of-keeping-obamacare

La gran muralla de Trump

Trump has always been a keen builder of walls, as this tweet from 2009 indicates:

@realDonaldTrump 12 May 2009
"My persona will never be that of a wallflower
– I'd rather build walls than cling to them"
– Donald J. Trump

One of Trump's most ambitious campaign promises was to build a wall along the US/Mexico border. Politicians often use construction terms as metaphors for their policies, often talking about building bridges, walls and roads as an easy-to-digest metaphor for economic progress, security and diplomacy. But Trump literally wants to build a big wall along the southern border. He sees a wall as the solution to a number of illegal immigration and drug trafficking problems that plague the states and cities along the US/Mexico border. There is evidence to suggest that this has always been a major ambition of his.

In 2014, the Department of Justice's annual report on crime statistics for the 2013 fiscal year reported that 38% of crimes identified an immigrant as the perpetrator. The website judicialwatch.org, a conservative, non-partisan organisation that investigates and reports on all things government, wrote an article expressing concern over crime rates near the Mexican border.

Judicialwatch.org

Department of Justice annual statistics 2013

Of the 61,529 criminal cases initiated by federal prosecutors last fiscal year, more than 40% — or 24,746 — were filed in court districts neighboring the Mexican border.[50]

Around the same time as the Judicialwatch.org report, the website *breitbart.com*, a news source that Donald Trump frequently references, covered the story with the headline:

DOJ: Regions Near Mexico Border Most Crime Ridden in US[51]

On August 5, 2014 Trump tweeted:

> **@realDonaldTrump** 5 Aug 2014
> **SECURE THE BORDER! BUILD A WALL!**

One of the many responses to his tweet is this gem:

> **@FallSnowman** 5 Aug 2014
> **@3sticksCGCS @U2Kouklixa** @realDonaldTrump
> **Its not Mr Trumps responsibility to protect America. It's our president!**

It could be argued that Trump took this comment to heart. As President he is now building a wall to protect America. But as I have shown and will continue to show, Trump has a

---

50 http://www.judicialwatch.org/blog/2014/08/doj-report-nearly-half-fed-crimes-near-mexican-border/?utm_source=facebook&utm_medium=post&utm_campaign=080514

51 http://www.breitbart.com/texas/2014/08/06/doj-regions-near-mexico-border-most-crime-ridden-in-us

trend in his rhetoric which indicates that his policy ideas are an extension of views he has always held. In 2014 he demanded a wall be built along the US Southern border to stem the flow of illegal immigrants into the US. In 2011, Trump sat down with Piers Morgan on CNN and discussed the idea of running for president in 2012.[52] Donald Trump intended to run for President and intended to build a wall along the Southern border for a long time before mainstream media started to pay attention to what he tweeted.

@realDonaldTrump 8 Oct 2014
The fight against ISIS starts at our border. 'At least' 10 ISIS have been caught crossing the Mexico border. Build a wall!

@realDonaldTrump 5 Mar 2015
Mexico's court system corrupt. I want nothing to do with Mexico other than to build an impenetrable WALL and stop them from ripping off U.S.

With the pattern established. No one should have been surprised when he stated:

'I would build a great wall, and nobody builds walls better than me, believe me, and I'll build them very inexpensively, I will build a great, great wall on our southern border. And I will have Mexico pay for that wall.'[53]

@realDonaldTrump 2 Jul 2015
A country must enforce its borders. Respect for the rule of law is at our country's core. We must build a wall!

---

52   Daily Mail article including highlights from the last decade, quotes from 2011 regarding Trump running for President in 2012 included in the article: http://www.dailymail.co.uk/news/article-3445761/My-revealing-Donald-diaries-PIERS-MORGAN-s-intimate-conversations-Trump-offer-unrivalled-insight-man-soon-President.html

53   Trump presidential running speech, June 2015

@realDonaldTrump 14 Jul 2015
A nation without borders is no nation at all.
We must build a wall. Let's Make America Great Again!

@realDonaldTrump 25 Aug 2015
Jeb Bush just talked about my border proposal to build
a "fence." It's not a fence, Jeb, it's a WALL, and there's
a BIG difference!

@realDonaldTrump 31 Aug 2015
For those that don't think a wall (fence) works, why
don't they suggest taking down the fence around the
White House? Foolish people!

@naz548 25 Aug 2015
@realDonaldTrump @claytonswisher Fence vs. Wall:
Can we get more infantile than that?

@claytonswisher 25 Aug 2015
@naz548 @realDonaldTrump reminds me of Dennis
Ross during the 2nd intifada assuring congress how
Israel was only making a temporary "fence"

(Khalil Janshan (@naz547) is the Executive Director of
the Arab Centre in Washington DC and Clayton Swisher
(@claytonswisher) is an American journalist who is
currently employed as the Manager of Investigative
Journalism at the Al Jazeera Media Network.)

@realDonaldTrump 19 Nov 2015
Eight Syrians were just caught on the southern border
trying to get into the U.S. ISIS maybe? I told you so.
WE NEED A BIG & BEAUTIFUL WALL!

@realDonaldTrump 31 Aug 2016
Mexico will pay for the wall - 100%!
#MakeAmericaGreatAgain #ImWithYou

@advodude 31 Aug 2016
@realDonaldTrump **no. No they won't.**

Twitter user @advodude pointed towards a tweet by the President of Mexico:

@EPN August 31, 2016
Al inicio de la conversación con Donald Trump dejé claro que México no pagará por el muro.

— The tweet directly translated as:

@EPN August 31, 2016
At the beginning of the conversation with Donald Trump I made it clear that Mexico will not pay for the wall.

A few hours later, Trump tweeted his response:

@realDonaldTrump 1 Sep 2016
Mexico will pay for the wall!

In September 2016, Trump gave a speech in Arizona, where he outlined his policy on Immigration:

Number One: We will build a wall along the Southern Border.

On day one, we will begin working on an impenetrable physical wall on the southern border. We will use the best technology, including above-and below-ground sensors, towers, aerial surveillance and manpower to supplement the wall, find and dislocate tunnels, and keep out the criminal cartels, and Mexico will pay for the wall.[54]

@realDonaldTrump 8 Jan 2017
Dishonest media says Mexico won't be paying for the wall if they pay a little later so the wall can be built more quickly. Media is fake!

Regardless of where the funding will come from and when, on January 25, 2017, Trump signed the executive order: Border security and enforcement improvements. Highlights of the executive order, specifically in reference to the wall include:

Section 2a

Secure the southern border of the United States through the immediate construction of a physical wall on the southern border, monitored and supported by adequate personnel so as to prevent illegal immigration, drug and human trafficking, and acts of terrorism.[55]

Section 4b

Identify and, to the extent permitted by law, allocate all sources of Federal funds for the planning, designing, and constructing of a physical wall along the southern border.[56]

---

54 http://www.politico.com/story/2016/08/donald-trump-immigration-address-transcript-227614

55 https://www.whitehouse.gov/the-press-office/2017/01/25/executive-order-border-security-and-immigration-enforcement-improvements

56 https://www.whitehouse.gov/the-press-office/2017/01/25/executive-order-border-security-and-immigration-enforcement-improvements

Tweet
Tweet
Tweet
Tweet
Tweet
Tweet
Tweet
Tweet
Tweet
Tweet

From the Twitterverse: #TrumpTrends

What can be best described as an expression of freedom of speech and, possibly, a series of organised anti-Trump trolling hashtag campaigns by the enraged citizens of Planet Earth, many hashtags trended on Twitter throughout Trump's campaign. Here are some of the most engaging trends.

#TrumpNoir

Following a disagreement with Fox News's Megyn Kelly during the first Republican debate in August 2016, Donald Trump phoned in to *CNN Tonight with Don Lemon* to further defend himself. During the conversation with Don Lemon, Trump stated that Megyn had 'blood coming out of her eyes, blood coming out of her whatever'. In January 2017, US comedian Patton Oswalt started tweeting film titles that have been, for lack of a better word, Trumped. Tweeters of the #TrumpNoir hashtag referenced events which spanned his entire campaign as inspiration for their alternate film titles.

@pattonoswalt 13 Jan 2017
The Yuge Sleep #TrumpNoir

@MatthewGellert 13 Jan 2017
The Bigly Sleep #TrumpNoir

During the first US Presidential debate Donald Trump said he was going to cut taxes 'big league' but it sounded like 'bigly'.

@NutherFineMess 13 Jan 2017
#trumpnoir **I'm Singin' In The... Hey This Isn't RAIN !**

@GordonFBennett 13 Jan 2017
The Siberian Candidate #trumpnoir

@**SuzySandor** 13 Jan 2017
Trumpocracy #TrumpNoir

@**garmonbozia42** 13 Jan 2017
#TrumpNoir: **Blame Runner**

@**Floki2020** 13 Jan 2017
Trumpocalypse Now
The Horror, the horror...
#TrumpNoir

@**SkilledNapper** 13 Jan 2017
The Short Goodbye... To Healthcare #TrumpNoir

@**ColonelFKassad** 13 Jan 2017
GinaTown #TrumpNoir

A reference to Donald Trump's pronunciation
of the word 'China'.

@**GeorgeMonfils** 14 Jan 2017
Trump = **Lie - Deny - Repeat** #TrumpNoir
#NotMyPresident **NOT a person for** #WeThePeople

#ThingsTrumpThinkAreOverrated

There are two parts to this trend, the first is Donald Trump's knee-jerk response to criticism, which is to label people as 'overrated'. The following are people that Donald Trump thinks overrated:

@realDonaldTrump 15 Oct 2012
Barack Obama is not who you think he is. Most overrated politician in US history.

On the cusp of Obama's second election win.

@realDonaldTrump 3 May 2013
As I've said many times before, Jon Stewart @TheDailyShow is highly overrated.

@realDonaldTrump 30 May 2015
Jon Stewart is the most overrated joke on television. A wiseguy with no talent. Not smart, but convinces dopes he is! Fading out fast.

Trump consistently tagged Jon Stewart as overrated. His tweet in June 2015 was in response to Stewart's reaction to Trump's announcement that he was running for President.

@realDonaldTrump 5 Jun 2015
@krauthammer pretends to be a smart guy, but if you look at his record, he isn't. A dummy who is on too many Fox shows. An overrated clown!

In response to Charles Krauthammer's comment that Donald Trump's policies were 'not serious politics'.[57]

---

57   http://dailycaller.com/2015/07/06/not-serious-politics-krauthammer-dismisses-rodeo-clown-donald-trump

@realDonaldTrump 23 Sep 2015
Do you ever notice that lightweight @megynkelly constantly goes after me but when I hit back it is totally sexist. She is highly overrated!

Trump tweets about Megyn Kelly of 'bleeding from her eyes...' fame. Although, in this case, he thinks she is overrated a solid none months prior to their clash at the first Republican debate.

@realDonaldTrump 29 Aug 2016
Crooked Hillary's brainpower is highly overrated. Probably why her decision making is so bad or, as stated by Bernie S, she has BAD JUDGEMENT

@realDonaldTrump 20 Nov 2016
The cast and producers of Hamilton, which I hear is highly overrated, should immediately apologize to Mike Pence for their terrible behavior

In response to the cast of the Broadway show 'Hamilton' asking for Senator Mike Pence to uphold American values.

@realDonaldTrump 9 Jan 2017
Meryl Streep, one of the most over-rated actresses in Hollywood, doesn't know me but attacked last night at the Golden Globes. She is a...

Trump's comment about Meryl Streep triggered a massive response from the Twitter community. Users tweeted lists of things that they thought Donald Trump considered overrated.

@DJWiggins44 Jan 9 2017

1. Consent

2. SNL

3. Nepotism

4. Democracy

5. Popular vote

6. US Intel

7. Equality

8. Women

9. Minoritie

#ThingsTrumpThinkAreOverrated

@almaldo2 Jan 9 2017
#ThingsTrumpThinkAreOverrated:
global warming and Mexico.

@BrandanJR 9 Jan 2017

Spellcheck.

Factcheck.

Writing his tax check.

#ThingsTrumpThinkAreOverrated

@analisisMW 10 Jan 2017

#ThingsTrumpThinkAreOverrated

Megyn Kelly

"Hamilton"

The Daily Show

Jerry Seinfeld

Alec Baldwin

Anyone famous who thinks different.

@6kennedyz 10 Jan 2017
His favourite actress (Meryl Streep, he said so in 2015)
#ThingsTrumpThinkAreOverrated

In 2015, when asked if there were any actresses that he is particularly fond of, Trump named-checked the Oscar winner.

'Julia Roberts is terrific, and many others,' Trump told *The Hollywood Reporter*'s Janice Min, before adding, 'Meryl Streep is excellent; she's a fine person, too.'[58]

@mocsandsocks 10 Jan 2017
Adjectives that are not superlatives.
#ThingsTrumpThinkAreOverrated

@StaciAnn 10 Jan 2017
#ThingsTrumpThinkAreOverrated
Everything but himself

---

58 http://www.vanityfair.com/hollywood/2017/01/meryl-streep-donald-trump-golden-globes

@johnny_thiel 10 Jan 2017
Normal adult sized hands...
#ThingsTrumpThinkAreOverrated

@denitrocity 10 Jan 2017
#ThingsTrumpThinkAreOverrated
A background in politics

@mike_superb 10 Jan 2017
#ThingsTrumpThinkAreOverrated **that mexico wont pay for THE WALL**

#GoldenShowerGate

On January 11, 2017, Buzzfeed published an alleged intelligence report from a private intelligence firm that outlined a complex network of spying and intelligence sharing within the US political campaign machine, ultimately alleging Russia were trying to influence the outcome of the 2016 election. CNN also picked up on the story and published an article about the document Buzzfeed received.
Trump responded swiftly.

@realDonaldTrump 11 Jan 2017
FAKE NEWS - A TOTAL POLITICAL WITCH HUNT!

@realDonaldTrump 13 Jan 2017
Totally made up facts by sleazebag political operatives, both Democrats and Republicans - FAKE NEWS! Russia says nothing exists. Probably...

> @realDonaldTrump 13 Jan 2017
> released by "Intelligence" even knowing there is no proof, and never will be. My people will have a full report on hacking within 90 days!

Terms like fake news and dishonest media were not uncommon phrases to appear on Donald Trump's social media platforms during his campaign. At a press conference shortly after the document was published and reported on, Trump refused to acknowledge CNN and Buzzfeed. Later, Trump enforced his position.

> @realDonaldTrump 12 Jan 2017
> We had a great News Conference at Trump Tower today. A couple of FAKE NEWS organizations were there but the people truly get what's going on

> @realDonaldTrump 15 Jan 2017
> INTELLIGENCE INSIDERS NOW CLAIM THE TRUMP DOSSIER IS "A COMPLETE FRAUD!" @OANN

The day before Trump's inauguration several news articles reported that John Brennan — the outgoing CIA Chief — defended himself after being accused of leaking the dossier. In the manner the public have been taught by the media to expect from a spy, the outgoing CIA chief neither confirmed or denied the legitimacy of the information.

Weekly Standard

No, obviously Brennan didn't "leak" the dossier because as he says it had been circulating for months. It never saw the light of day because news outlets were incapable of verifying many of its claims. So how did a report once universally deemed dubious get out into the open?

What was leaked was not the dossier, but what the president-elect was briefed. What makes the leak appear to be part of an information campaign waged against the president-elect is that the dossier, as Brennan admitted, had been circulating for a long time.[59]

The sudden appearance of this report days before the inauguration, its poor quality, and reports indicating the British spy/author went into hiding meant most major news agencies ignored the story. It is hard to believe an intelligence report of this nature would get this far without anyone knowing about it and as far as news and politics goes, it was a non-event.

The twitterverse however loves a good conspiracy and a good pun. The dossier contained some very interesting reports on moles and cyberattacks orchestrated by Russia. Parts of it sound like it was lifted from a Tom Clancy novel. Twitter users chose to ignore the thriller-esque content and focus on more unbelievable and seedier claims about Trump.

The hashtag #GoldenShowerGate spawned some classic one liners from the tweeting masses.

@JamesWHarrison 10 Jan 2017
I guess this puts a whole new meaning to the phrase "leaked intelligence". #goldenshowergate

@Bords94 10 Jan 2017
Guys he's not even our president yet and we already have #goldenshowergate

@keithboykin 11 Jan 2017
The man who rose to political power spreading a fake news scandal about Obama says he is a victim of a fake news scandal. #GoldenShowerGate

---

59 http://www.weeklystandard.com/brennan-the-russian-dossier-and-obamas-grand-political-strategy/article/2006369

@**JoshNoneYaBiz** 11 Jan 2017
Anyone who fell for this, urine idiot.
#GoldenShowerGate

Google analytics reported a rise in popularity of people searching the term 'Golden Shower', which would indicate that not only did the latest Trump controversy trend on Twitter but that a large proportion of Google users now know what the fetish term 'Golden Shower' actually means.

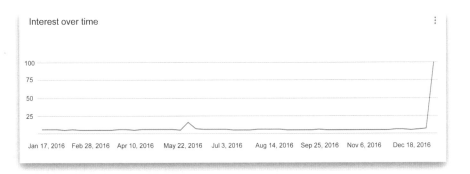

In a final satirical twist, the inauguration included what can only be described as a form of state censorship as the word 'Don' in the porta-potties company 'Don's Johns' was covered in blue tape.

@**black_swan_1984** 15 Jan 2017
#Inauguration **irregularity: Porta-potties bearing 'Don' taped over** @**CNNPolitics** cnn.it/2jNJntL #donjohn #GoldenShowerGate #resist

CNN

Inauguration irregularity: Porta-potties bearing 'Don' taped over

Inauguration planners rushed to wipe away a potential controversy Friday after porta-potties on the National Mall happened to be adorned with the President-elect's first name.

Workers were spotted Friday morning covering the "Don's Johns" logo with blue masking tape.[60]

---

60   http://edition.cnn.com/2017/01/13/politics/donald-trump-inauguration-porta-potties/index.html

September 2016: Conflict and terror

September will always to be a BIG month in US politics, especially in an election year. September 2016 marked 15 years since the destruction of the World Trade Center in New York City. Whether Trump was responding to attacks in New York, past and present, or firebombing a particularly troublesome news agency, September 2016 had a distinctive conflict orientated narrative.

Trump tackles terror

September 11, 2016 (9/11). On the day, Trump issued a statement on Facebook:

> 'Today is a day of sadness and remembrance. It is also a day of resolve. Our solemn duty on behalf of all those who perished that September day 15 years ago, is to work together as one nation to keep all of our people safe from an enemy that seeks nothing less than to destroy our way of life.'[61]

This is not uncharacteristic behaviour.

@realDonaldTrump 11 Sep 2015
Let's all take a moment to remember all of the heroes from a very tragic day that we cannot let happen again!

@realDonaldTrump 11 Sep 2014
They should have rebuilt the two buildings of the World Trade Center exactly as they were, except taller and stronger. A better statement!

---

61   Excerpt from Donald Trump's Facebook statement about 9/11:
      https://www.facebook.com/DonaldTrump

@realDonaldTrump 11 Sep 2013
**God bless all the brave souls who perished 12 years
ago today. You will never be forgotten!**

By comparison, Hillary Clinton attended a remembrance
ceremony in the city of New York, but left early for
health issues.

Later in the month, there were a series of bombings
in New York:

@realDonaldTrump 18 Sep 2016
**I would like to express my warmest regards, best
wishes and condolences to all of the families and
victims of the horrible bombing in NYC.**

When the bombing happened, both Donald Trump and Hillary
Clinton were flying to their next campaign city; they were
briefed and both commented to the press at the next
available moment.

Donald Trump called a press conference to say:

> *'I must tell you that just before I got off the plane a bomb
> went off in New York and nobody knows what's going on.'*

Hillary Clinton also held a press conference, she said:

> *'I've been briefed about bombings in New York and New
> Jersey, and the attacks in Minnesota, obviously we need
> to do everything we can to support our first responders.'*

The words both candidates communicated are very similar but
their rhetoric is quite different. It is true that both candidates
used the word bomb or bombing to describe the incident but
while Hillary Clinton conveyed that a terrible incident had
happened but more information is needed, Trump's language
was much more aggressive and suggested a sense of
panic and confusion.

Given that Trump employs plain-speaking to relate to his voters and to project himself as the heart and voice of the people, his language is on par with how people would probably feel about an incident such as an explosion in New York, a week after the 9/11 remembrance ceremony.

@realDonaldTrump 19 Sep 2016
Terrible attacks in NY, NJ and MN this weekend. Thinking of victims, their families and all Americans! We need to be strong!

Even though Trump was ahead in the polls at this point, his decision to play the 'unity in the face of terrorism' card was a gamble.

The Guardian

Chris Christie, the Republican governor of New Jersey, later praised Donald Trump for his bold stance from the beginning:

"I think that what Donald did was perfectly appropriate to tell that group in Colorado Springs that a bomb had exploded," Christie said.

"I don't think you have to defer when saying that there was an explosion and a bomb in New York. I mean, everybody knew that. It was being reported on television."[62]

The gamble paid off but had the incident turned out to be nothing, the media response to Trump would have been much different.

---

62   https://www.theguardian.com/us-news/2016/sep/18/clinton-trump-new-york-bombing

September 24

CNN

Washington mall shooting: Manhunt underway after gunman kills 5

A man carrying a rifle entered a Macy's store at a mall in Washington state, shot dead four women and a man, and vanished into the night, police said.[63]

CNN (update of the story)

Washington mall shooting: Police arrest 20-year-old suspect

One day after a shooting left five people dead at a mall north of Seattle, authorities arrested a 20-year-old suspect Saturday after an overnight manhunt that left the city on edge.

Arcan Cetin is suspected of killing four women and a man Friday night at the Cascade Mall in Burlington, Washington.

Washington state authorities said it's too early to rule out terrorism or anything else because their investigation is still in the preliminary stages.

Before the suspect's arrest, an official with the FBI had told reporters there was "no evidence at this time" of a link to terrorism.[64]

---

63   http://edition.cnn.com/2016/09/23/us/washington-mall-shooting

64   http://edition.cnn.com/2016/09/24/us/washington-mall-shooting

@realDonaldTrump 26 Sep 2016
Five people killed in Washington State by a Middle Eastern immigrant. Many people died this weekend in Ohio from drug overdoses. N.C. riots!

Trump's choice of words is critical; the gunman, Arcan Cetin, had emigrated from Turkey, legally, and is a US citizen. While it may be true that Turkey is part of the Middle East, broad geographical terms like Middle Eastern, Westerner and Asian are often employed by the media and politicians to illicit a specific emotional response after an event. If Trump had said 'a Turkish immigrant' or 'a Turkish-born US citizen' or 'a US citizen who emigrated from the Middle East', it is likely that the emotional response to the fact would have had less impact and would have been a less effective vehicle to push his anti-immigration policies.

Trump's war on news: CNN

Looking back at Donald Trump's Twitter feed, it is easy to see that the Trump/CNN relationship goes through good and bad patches:

@realDonaldTrump 11 Sep 2012
Discussing the 9/11 attack and coverage with @kingsthings while hosting the 25th anniversary of his @CNN show

@realDonaldTrump 28 Jun 2013
Congratulations to @newtgingrich on being signed to co-host @CNN Crossfire. Great move by Jeff Zucker.

@realDonaldTrump 4 Apr 2014
I hate what has happened to the once great @CNN.

@realDonaldTrump 18 Jul 2015
The $10 billion (net worth) is **AFTER** all debt and liabilities. So simple to understand but @CNN & @CNNPolitics is just plain dumb!

Throughout his campaign for election, Donald Trump's remarks about CNN have became increasingly aggressive and hostile.

@realDonaldTrump 16 Sep 2015
Will be heading over to the debate soon.
Can you believe @CNN is "milking" it for almost 3 hours? Too long, too many people on stage!

@realDonaldTrump 5 Jun 2016
I am watching @CNN very little lately because they are so biased against me. Shows are predictable garbage! CNN and MSM is one big lie!

In September 2016, Trump seemed hell bent on discrediting CNN.

@realDonaldTrump 3 Sep 2016
Great visit to Detroit church, fantastic reception, and all @CNN talks about is a small protest outside. Inside a large and wonderful crowd!

@realDonaldTrump 9 Sep 2016
@CNN is unwatchable. Their news on me is fiction. They are a disgrace to the broadcasting industry and an arm of the Clinton campaign.

@realDonaldTrump 17 Sep 2016
@CNN just doesn't get it, and that's why their ratings are so low - and getting worse. Boring anti-Trump panelists, mostly losers in life!

@realDonaldTrump 26 Sep 2016
Wow, did great in the debate polls (except for
@CNN - which I don't watch). Thank you!

@realDonaldTrump 29 Sep 2016
Wow, did you see how badly @CNN (Clinton News
Network) is doing in the ratings. With people like
@donlemon, who could expect any more?

Donald Trump does not hide that he likes to fight his enemies. Almost anyone or any organisation that spoke out against him during his campaign was branded as a Hillary flunky or accused of generating biased or fake news stories.

Whether or not CNN leans slightly left in their political reporting is irrelevant, unbiased news networks are hard to come by and most people understand that the way a story is reported varies from news network to news network. What made Donald Trump's attack on CNN seem disproportionate is his approach when dealing with Fox News.

Fox News is very right-leaning and does not try to hide it. Donald Trump likes Fox News and does not hide it.

@realDonaldTrump 13 Jun 2016
I am watching @FoxNews and how fairly they are
treating me and my words, and @CNN, and the total
distortion of my words and what I am saying

@realDonaldTrump 4 Oct 2016
Wow, @CNN is so negative. Their panel is a joke,
biased and very dumb. I'm turning to @FoxNews
where we get a fair shake! Mike will do great

China

An article in *The Australian* from early January 2017 is a good jumping off point to begin an analysis of Trump's relationship with China.

The Australian

Donald Trump, China tensions risk armed conflict

China didn't invent the brand of mercantilism that Donald Trump rails against; it copied the playbook from its neighbours. Japan grew rich by promoting exports while protecting its own industries. So did South Korea. They both manipulated their currencies and showered favours on politically connected business cartels, skewing domestic competition.

But here's one major difference: these trading powerhouses together with Taiwan, Singapore and others in Asia who aggressively pursued export and investment-led growth were friends and allies of the US, whereas China is a strategic competitor and military rival.[65]

In the years leading up to his campaign for the presidency Trump regularly tweeted his feelings about China and what China was doing. For example, with regards to the search for flight MH370 that mysteriously disappeared in March 2014:

@realDonaldTrump 20 Mar 2014
We're spending a fortune looking for the lost plane with mostly Chinese passengers, and that's OK-but how much are Russia & China spending?

---

65   http://www.theaustralian.com.au/business/wall-street-journal/donald-trump-china-tensions-risk-armed-conflict/news-story/1cd14e4388f82ff01ce37b14d89b08f8

@realDonaldTrump 20 May 2014
A classic - China just signs massive oil and gas deal with Russia giving Russia plenty of ammo to continue laughing in U.S. face.

@realDonaldTrump 20 May 2014
Remember, China is not a friend of the United States!

@realDonaldTrump 5 Sep 2014
China is going to complete 59 new theme parks by 2020, over $23B in expansion. That would take over 100 years in our country.

Trump referenced China during his presidency announcement:

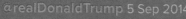

'Our country is in serious trouble. We don't have victories anymore. We used to have victories, but we don't have them. When was the last time anybody saw us beating, let's say, China in a trade deal? They kill us. I beat China all the time. All the time.'

Jobs and economy are a theme of modern political campaigns; people always want jobs and more money. Given the stance Trump has taken regarding the status of the US economy, it is unsurprising that he viewed China as a direct competitor. The US and China are number one and two when it comes to countries in order of GDP.

@realDonaldTrump 20 May 2016
Crooked Hillary has zero imagination and even less stamina. ISIS, China, Russia and all would love for her to be president. 4 more years!

In early December 2016, in a move whose only purpose seems to be antagonising both the (then) Obama government and Beijing, Trump spoke to the Prime Minister of Taiwan over the phone, and tweeted about it.

The China/Taiwan/US relationship is tricky and some political history is required to understand the possible implications of Trump's actions.

China: A brief history of the China/Taiwan/US triangle

In 1949, the Civil war between the Republic of China (ROC) and the People's Republic of China (PRC) ended with the PRC substantiating their position as the ruling government of China and its territories. The previous government, the ROC, fled to Taiwan where it continued to govern and proclaim itself as the legitimate government of China.

As of January 2017, the PRC is recognised as the legitimate government of China and while officially Taiwan is part of China, it's a largely democratic government. Commercial and industrial sufficiencies and repeated claims for independence means that most of the world unofficially recognises Taiwan's independence through non-diplomatic channels such as weapon sales and other economic ventures.

Looking at Donald Trump's pre-election campaign tweets, it is clear that he is aware of the political situation.

BBC
September 2011

China hits out at US deal on Taiwan F-16 fighters

China has reacted angrily to a US deal to upgrade Taiwan's ageing fleet of US-built F-16 fighter planes.

Vice-Foreign Minister Zhang Zhijun said the $5.85bn (£3.77bn) deal would "inevitably undermine bilateral relations", including military and security co-operation.[66]

@realDonaldTrump 18 Oct 2011
@BarackObama is holding Taiwan's request for 66 advanced F-16's. Wrong message to send to China.

@realDonaldTrump 18 Nov 2011
Why is @BarackObama delaying the sale of F-16 aircraft to Taiwan? Wrong message to send to China. #TimeToGetTough

The US sold Taiwan weapons as a means of maintaining the balance of power in East Asia. The fear is that if China was to aggressively take back Taiwan it would destabilise the region and lead to conflict and/or a rapid expansion of China's territory.

BBC

"China traditionally reacts strongly to US military co-operation with Taiwan, which it considers its territory.

Last year, when the US sold missiles and other hardware to Taiwan, China suspended military exchanges with the US."[67]

---

66   http://www.bbc.com/news/world-asia-pacific-15014358

67   http://www.bbc.com/news/world-asia-pacific-15014358

Reuters

U.S. seeks to reassure Beijing after Trump call with Taiwan leader

The White House said on Monday it had sought to reassure China after President-elect Donald Trump's phone call with Taiwan's leader last week, which the Obama administration warned could undermine progress in relations with Beijing.

The statement from a spokesman for U.S. President Barack Obama highlighted concerns about the potential fallout from Trump's unusual call with Taiwan President Tsai Ing-wen on Friday, which prompted a diplomatic protest from Beijing on Saturday.

White House spokesman Josh Earnest said senior National Security Council officials spoke twice with Chinese officials over the weekend to reassure them of Washington's commitment to the "One China" policy and to "reiterate and clarify the continued commitment of the United States to our longstanding China policy."[68]

@realDonaldTrump 3 Dec 2016
Interesting how the U.S. sells Taiwan billions of dollars of military equipment but I should not accept a congratulatory call.

The Yuan and the Dollar

Trump stated in his 'contract with the American voter', which is an outline of his aims during his first 100 days in office, that he will 'direct the Secretary of the Treasury to label China a currency manipulator'.

---

68   http://www.reuters.com/article/us-usa-trump-china-idUSKBN13T0SQ

There is a level of certainty that the investigation triggered by this instruction will find that China is indeed manipulating its currency. If China was asked to adjust their financial habits and 'fix' the economic imbalance, whether they would comply or not is an unknown factor.

Presidential candidate Mitt Romney made a similar campaign promise in 2013. Bloomberg ran a story hypothesising the outcome if 'President Romney' had followed through.

Bloomberg

Calling China a Currency Manipulator Could Be Empty Gesture

Imagine it's Jan. 21, 2013, the day after Mitt Romney's inauguration. He arrives at the Oval Office for his first full day as president, and makes good on a major campaign promise: He signs an executive order declaring China a currency manipulator.

What happens next? Not a whole lot.

There is no doubt that China would meet the tests in the law. The U.S. ran a $295.4 billion trade deficit with China last year, an 8.2 percent increase above the 2010 level. Allowing the yuan to appreciate would make Chinese goods more expensive for U.S. consumers, reducing U.S. imports of Chinese merchandise. But how would the Treasury secretary "ensure" China adjusts its currency accordingly, when China holds almost $1 trillion in U.S. government debt?
The answer: It could not.

What little leverage the U.S. has over China will disappear if Romney approves the manipulator moniker, an act that China will interpret as an attack. This helps explain why, under President Barack Obama, the U.S. has refrained from doing so. Instead, Obama and Treasury Secretary Timothy

Geithner have opted to negotiate, mostly behind the scenes, with China.[69]

US/China relations are sensitive and it is possible that any aggressive action by Trump against China could be interpreted as hostile.

Expanding horizons

Trump's China/economy campaign promises could be the tip of the iceberg for some titanically proportioned China/ US politics over the next four years, especially if we consider the sore point of China's gradual expansion of territory in the South China Sea.

@realDonaldTrump 4 Dec 2016
Did China ask us if it was OK to devalue their currency (making it hard for our companies to compete), heavily tax our products going into.

@realDonaldTrump 4 Dec 2016
their country (the U.S. doesn't tax them) or to build a massive military complex in the middle of the South China Sea? I don't think so!

ABC News
15 December

South China Sea: Satellite images appear to show weapons systems on artificial islands

---

69   https://www.bloomberg.com/view/articles/2012-10-17/calling-china-a-currency-manipulator-could-be-empty-gesture

@realDonaldTrump 17 Dec 2016

China steals United States Navy research drone in international waters - rips it out of water and takes it to China in unprecedented act.

@realDonaldTrump 18 Dec 2016

We should tell China that we don't want the drone they stole back.- let them keep it!

Around the Inauguration ABC News reported on a story about Australia's concern about a potential US/China conflict.

ABC News

South China Sea: Australia in firing line if US and China go to war, experts warn

The incoming US President looms as critical. The South China Sea may just be the biggest flashpoint of Trump's presidency. He has already said that China needs to be taught to respect the US and observers say it remains unknown just how he would react to a confrontation with Beijing.

Mr Brown is a former Army officer who led troops into combat in Iraq. Now, he works from a desk contemplating the worst case scenarios.

"We don't know how Trump would handle some sort of conflict scenario with China or in Asia. We know that some members of his team have sharp views on China taking a more assertive approach. They point to the fact that Obama really got pushed around by China in the last eight years," Mr Brown said.[70]

As of the end of January 2017, Trump had not yet enacted his China plan.

---

70   http://www.abc.net.au/news/2017-01-20/australia-firing-line-if-the-us-and-china-go-to-war-experts/8198544

Global warming

@realDonaldTrump 9 Sep 2014
Windmills are the greatest threat in the US to both bald and golden eagles. Media claims fictional 'global warming' is worse.

@realDonaldTrump 15 Jul 2014
They only changed the term to CLIMATE CHANGE when the words GLOBAL WARMING didn't work anymore. Come on people, get smart!

@realDonaldTrump 29 Jul 2014
It's late in July and it is really cold outside in New York. Where the hell is GLOBAL WARMING??? We need some fast! It's now CLIMATE CHANGE

Trump's opinion of global warming/climate change is very clear; he doesn't believe in it, he thinks it is a fiction, a joke. By contrast, the Obama administration was very concerned with climate change. In November 2015, *The Guardian* reported on President Obama's veto of the Keystone XL oil pipeline project; if President Obama had not vetoed the bill it would have become law. The newspaper quoted Obama as saying:

> *'America is now a global leader when it comes to taking serious action to fight climate change. And frankly, approving this project would have undercut that global leadership.'*[71]

A lack of policy relating to the Global concerns of climate change is not unexpected given Trump's stance on the subject. If, however, climate change is a genuine issue then Trump's efforts to stimulate the US economy with projects directly

---

71   https://www.theguardian.com/environment/2015/nov/07/keystone-xl-pipeline-rejection-signals-us-lead-climate-change

related to fossil fuel production and transportation will counter the work of the previous administration and the global community.

Meanwhile in Obama-land

On August 26, 2016, a number of newspapers reported that President Obama had signed an executive order to expand the protected zone around a rare archipelago near Hawaii:

The Telegraph

The American President yesterday signed an executive order quadrupling the protective perimeter around Papahānaumokuākea, an archipelago off the coast of his native Hawaii that is home to some of the oldest and most unusual creatures on the planet.

The archipelago was first designated a protected Marine National Monument a decade ago by President George W Bush. But deep sea drilling and commercial fishing close to the area had placed the ecosystems there under threat once again.[72]

In November of the same year, the media began to speculate that Trump's economic plan could be damaging to the environment.

The Economist

Mr Trump may kick into reverse a process of globalisation which had already stalled. That will not restore to workers a golden age of prosperity and security. Instead, it will increase the extent to which the global economy feels like a zero-sum competition, increasing the risk of political conflict.[73]

While Trump's drive to increase the number of jobs in industries such as manufacturing and coal production was key to his strategy to secure the presidency, the US is the second

---

72   http://www.telegraph.co.uk/news/2016/08/26/looking-to-his-legacy-barack-obama-creates-largest-protected-nat

73   http://www.economist.com/blogs/freeexchange/2016/11/global-economy

highest producer of CO^2 emissions in the world, second only to China.

At this point, the US was weeks away from ratifying the Paris Accord agreement on climate change, which would require the US to reduce CO^2 emissions and reduce the volume of industry that use fossil fuels as well as invest in green energy initiatives.

A Trump tweet from 2012 linked 'fictitious climate change' and China via a for global economic domination.

@realDonaldTrump 6 Nov 2012
The concept of global warming was created by and for the Chinese in order to make U.S. manufacturing non-competitive.

While Trump has been consistent with his opinions on immigration, terrorism and healthcare over the years, during the 2016 election there was an indication that Trump still held this opinion on global warming, which may explain his lack of green-policies.

Trump's contract

In Trump's 'Contract with the American voter', his 'seven actions to protect American workers' includes:

> **I will lift the restrictions on the production of $50 trillion dollars' worth of job-producing American energy reserves, including shale, oil, natural gas and clean coal.**

> **Lift the Obama-Clinton roadblocks and allow vital energy infrastructure projects, like the Keystone Pipeline, to move forward.**

> **Cancel billions in payments to U.N. climate change programs and use the money to America's water and environmental infrastructure.[74]**

---

74 https://assets.donaldjtrump.com/_landings/contract/O-TRU-102316-Contractv02.pdf

@realDonaldTrump 19 Oct 2015
It's really cold outside, they are calling it a major freeze, weeks ahead of normal. Man, we could use a big fat dose of global warming!

Trump's plan to ditch all things climate change and develop the industries that are often considered to be at the centre of the issue could have global political implications. The groundbreaking Paris Accord is extremely fragile and if the US pulls away from all climate change initiatives, this sentiment could generate political ripples around the globe.

Rex Tillerson, who was CEO of ExxonMobil until he was appointed Secretary of State by President Trump, would be the person in front of the camera if Trump decides to reverse the previous government's decision on the Paris Accord and other climate change policies.

Being the former CEO of a global petroleum company, it is difficult to imagine Mr Tillerson offering much resistance to Trump's plans to scrap climate change in favour of fossil fuel production.

In early 2017, a number of US firms who see a future in low-carbon technologies urged Donald Trump to reconsider his position on climate change as an anti-climate position could have significant economic impacts in the US.

The Independent

Donald Trump urged to ditch his climate change denial by 630 major firms who warn it 'puts American prosperity at risk'

'We want the US economy to be energy efficient and powered by low-carbon energy'.[75]

---

75   http://www.independent.co.uk/news/world/americas/donald-trump-climate-change-science-denial-global-warming-630-major-companies-put-american-a7519626.html

Note: At the end of January 2017, we know that Trump is planning to go ahead with the Keystone XL oil pipeline.

It is also worth noting that although I have focused on the environmental impact of the Keystone XL pipeline, there is also a sovereignty issue as the pipeline runs very close to Rosebud Sioux Indian territory. Representatives of the Rosebud Sioux tribe vowed to take legal action if the pipeline went ahead.[76]

October: Sex, likes, and a rogue candidate

The VP debate

The Vice Presidential debate between Mike Pence (R) and
Tim Kaine (D) took place on October 4, 2016 in Farmville,
Virginia. Trump twisted the throttle on his social media
machine and live tweeted commentary throughout
the debate.

The build-up

@realDonaldTrump 4 Oct 2016
**I will be watching the great Governor @Mike_Pence
and live tweeting the VP debate tonight starting at
8:30pm est! Enjoy!**

@realDonaldTrump 5 Oct 2016
Here we go - Enjoy!

@realDonaldTrump 5 Oct 2016
Both are looking good! Now we begin!

@realDonaldTrump 5 Oct 2016
**Wow, @CNN is so negative. Their panel is a joke,
biased and very dumb. I'm turning to @FoxNews
where we get a fair shake! Mike will do great**

@realDonaldTrump 5 Oct 2016
**@megynkelly - I am in Nevada. Sorry to inform you
Kellyanne is in the audience. Better luck next time.**

The debate begins

Trump praised Pence and criticised Kaine all through the debate:

@realDonaldTrump 5 Oct 2016
@mike_pence is doing a great job - so far, no contest!

@realDonaldTrump 5 Oct 2016
ICYMI: PENCE: I RAN A STATE THAT WORKED; KAINE RAN A STATE THAT FAILED.

What could be viewed as a progression in his social media campaign, Trump chose to use the comments he received from his supporters on twitter to express more risqué commentary.

@realDonaldTrump 5 Oct 2016
"@RoadkingL: @mike_pence Wow, Kaine couldn't go 12 seconds without a lie. Marines and military are scared of the liar running. #bengazi"

@realDonaldTrump 5 Oct 2016
"@lainey34210: @realDonaldTrump Great opening Pence" Donald J. Trump

@realDonaldTrump 5 Oct 2016
"@elisac006: @nycmia @realDonaldTrump I agree. Kaine looks like a fool!!"

@realDonaldTrump 5 Oct 2016
"@Jnelson52722: @realDonaldTrump @Susiesentinel Kaine looks like an evil crook out of the Batman movies"

@realDonaldTrump 5 Oct 2016
"@ARSenMissyIrvin: I want a "you're fired" president with people in Govt who are WASTING my tax $'s."

@realDonaldTrump 5 Oct 2016
"@ifdanyt: @realDonaldTrump Loving @mike_pence he's so likeable and sensible. Kaine is just talking bull!

@realDonaldTrump 5 Oct 2016
@mike_pence and I will defeat #ISIS. bit.ly/2dl98dg #VPDebate

@realDonaldTrump 5 Oct 2016
Mike Pence won big. We should all be proud of Mike!

@realDonaldTrump 5 Oct 2016
The constant interruptions last night by Tim Kaine should not have been allowed. Mike Pence won big!

Hillary Clinton also tweeted during the debate:

@HillaryClinton 5 Oct 2016
"We trust American women."

@HillaryClinton 5 Oct 2016
Thank you, @TimKaine. #VPDebate

@HillaryClinton 5 Oct 2016
"We support Roe v. Wade. We support the constitutional right of American women to... make their own decision about pregnancy."
— @timkaine

Sexual scandals threaten to derail Trump

On October 10, 2016, mainstream media released an audio recording of Donald Trump from 2005. In the recording he described his sexual conduct towards women. The release of the footage sent ripples through the Republican Party and a number of Republicans withdrew their support for Trump.

The Guardian

'You can do anything': Trump brags on tape about using fame to get women

…Meanwhile the list of Republicans withdrawing their support from Trump was growing.

Trump had been scheduled to appear with the House speaker, Paul Ryan, at a Republican event in Wisconsin on Saturday, his first appearance on the campaign trail with the most powerful elected Republican official. But Ryan said late on Friday that Trump would no longer be in attendance.

Ryan released a statement on Friday night saying: "I am sickened by what I heard today. Women are to be championed and revered, not objectified. I hope Mr Trump treats this situation with the seriousness it deserves and works to demonstrate to the country that he has greater respect for women than this clip suggests."

On Friday night Jason Chaffetz, the chair of the House oversight committee, declared that he would not vote for Trump. The Utah congressman joined his state's governor, Gary Herbert, in abandoning Trump in the aftermath of his remarks.

Chaffetz, who sounded beside himself with anger in an interview with CNN, said he could not face his wife and 15-year-old daughter if he continued to support Trump.

He said Trump had not properly apologised for his lewd remarks and had only expressed regret for "getting caught".[77]

Hillary Clinton capitalised on the moment and used it to push her 'not this man for President' narrative:

> **@HillaryClinton** 7 Oct 2016
> **This is horrific. We cannot allow this man to become president.**

Trump issued a statement explaining his words and justifying his position to continue to run as the Presidential nominee for the Republican Party.

> *'I've never said I am a perfect person, nor pretended to be someone that I am not. I've said and done things I regret and the words released today on this more than decade-old video are one of them.*
>
> *'...I pledge to be a better man tomorrow and will never ever let you down.*
>
> *'...Let's be honest, we are living in the real world. This is nothing more than a distraction from the important issues we are facing today.'*[78]

Trump, after beginning to sound quite Presidential retaliates against the previous government and the Clintons:

> *'We are losing our jobs, we are less safe than we were eight years ago and Washington is totally broken. Hillary Clinton and her kind has run our country into the ground.'*

---

77   https://www.theguardian.com/us-news/2016/oct/07/donald-trump-leaked-recording-women

78   https://www.theguardian.com/us-news/2016/oct/07/donald-trump-leaked-recording-women

@realDonaldTrump 8 Oct 2016
Certainly has been an interesting 24 hours!

@realDonaldTrump 8 Oct 2016
The media and establishment want me out of the race so badly - I WILL NEVER DROP OUT OF THE RACE, WILL NEVER LET MY SUPPORTERS DOWN! #MAGA

@realDonaldTrump 9 Oct 2016
Tremendous support (except for some Republican "leadership"). Thank you.

A few of days later, and moments before the Presidential debate:

@realDonaldTrump 9 Oct 2016
Join me on #FacebookLive **as I conclude my final** #debate **preparations.**

What followed was a live-streamed press conference. Trump framed the press conference within 'final debate preparations'.

Trump and four women sat in front of the press. These four women were allegorical of the female component of Trump supporters, they looked like normal, everyday people. Each woman stated why she believed in Donald Trump.

The third woman to speak, Juanita Broaddrick had recently been retweeted by Trump when she commented on the 2005 recording.

@atensnut **retweeted by** @realDonaldTrump
8 Oct 2016 **Hillary calls Trump's remarks "horrific" while she lives with and protects a "Rapist". Her actions are horrific.**

@atensnut retweeted by @realDonaldTrump
8 Oct 2016 How many times must it be said?
Actions speak louder than words. DT said bad things!
HRC threatened me after BC raped me.

During the press conference Ms Broddrick said:

'I tweeted recently and Mr Trump retweeted it, that
action speaks louder than words. Mr Trump may have
said some bad words but Bill Clinton raped me and
Hillary Clinton threatened me. I don't think there is
any comparison.'[79]

In terms of media sensationalism and public reaction, the
tweets and live Facebook press conference can be viewed,
analytically, in a similar vein to 'Golden Shower Gate'.
Whether the allegations are true or false, the media hype
around it created discussion amongst the voters which
distracted people from the original event, with the volume
of controversy generated during the 2016 campaign, any
sort of distraction from the more slanderous statements
associated with Donald Trump were only ever going to help
him win the presidency.

@realDonaldTrump 9 Oct 2016
"@CharleneOsbor17: @realDonaldTrump **politicians**
don't count. It's the people. We are behind trump all
the way to White House."

Usually when Trump tweets something defamatory against
his opponents or makes an enthusiastic claim on the White
House, Twitter responds with mockery and disgust, but the
bulk of the responses, this time, are pro-Trump and very anti-
Hillary, proof that Trump's distraction worked.

---

79   https://www.facebook.com/DonaldTrump/videos/10157857037430725/

@realDonaldTrump 9 Oct 2016
"@eericmyers: @realDonaldTrump "Republican leadership" should have only one job: Help elect the nominee we voted for, Donald J. Trump."

@realDonaldTrump 9 Oct 2016
"@maidaa17: @realDonaldTrump GOP traitors! Not supporting U is voting for her, destroying America."

Trump goes rogue

Despite handling the 2005 sexual scandal recording well and managing to distract the public with a rape accusation against Bill Clinton, Trump's popularity dropped in the polls, if only briefly.

Time Magazine

Hillary Clinton now leads Donald Trump by eight points among likely voters, according to a national tracking poll released Wednesday.

The new Reuters/Ipsos poll shows that after Sunday's second presidential debate and the leaked video of lewd comments he made regarding women in 2005, Republican voters are in a tight spot.[80]

Politicians read this dip as the end of the 'Donald Trump' adventure and distanced themselves from him, in an attempt to save face with the Party and potentially secure a spot as the new Republican Party candidate if the GOP found themselves in a position where they need to replace Trump.
Trump fought back.

---

80   http://www.time.com/4527825/poll-hillary-clinton-donald-trump-post-debate

@realDonaldTrump 9 Oct 2016
Tremendous support (except for some Republican "leadership"). Thank you.

@realDonaldTrump 9 Oct 2016
So many self-righteous hypocrites. Watch their poll numbers - and elections - go down!

@realDonaldTrump 10 Oct 2016
Paul Ryan should spend more time on balancing the budget, jobs and illegal immigration and not waste his time on fighting Republican nominee Donald J. Trump

@realDonaldTrump 11 Oct 2016
Despite winning the second debate in a landslide (every poll), it is hard to do well when Paul Ryan and others give zero support!

With momentum behind his anti-Republican tweeting rage, Trump drew a line in the sand and indicted that he would be prepared to run independently, that he did not need the backing of the GOP to secure the presidency.

@realDonaldTrump 11 Oct 2016
It is so nice that the shackles have been taken off me and I can now fight for America the way I want to.

@realDonaldTrump 11 Oct 2016
With the exception of cheating Bernie out of the nom the Dems have always proven to be far more loyal to each other than the Republicans!

@realDonaldTrump 11 Oct 2016
Disloyal R's are far more difficult than Crooked Hillary. They come at you from all sides. They don't know how to win - I will teach them!

Despite the minor dip in polling popularity and the apparent exodus of support, Trump continued to run as the Republican candidate.

#MAGA
#InaugurationDay
#AmericaFirst
#MAGA
#MAGA
#MAGA
#RIGGED
#MAGA
#DrainTheSwamp
#BigLeagueTruth
#AmericaFirst
#TrumpPence16
#TeamTrump
#RepealObamacare
#MakeAmericaGreatAgain
#MAGA

Hashtag policy

Throughout Donald Trump's campaign, he embraced hashtag culture and used it to promote a number of his key policies. This chapter will look at some of his key hashtag trends in terms of what policy they represented and how he used social media to communicate details.

#DrainTheSwamp

Originally coined as a political metaphor by Winfield R Gaylord, an American politician who belonged to the Socialist Party of America in the very early 1900s. For Winfred the phrase represented the Socialist's desire to 'drain' the 'capitalist swamp'.

The phrase resurfaced a number of times in US political history and was always used as a bureaucratic metaphor for government reform or to remove an aspect of government that is considered unethical. Donald Rumsfeld coined the term following the September 11 World Trade Center attacks.

CNN

Rumsfeld: U.S. must 'drain the swamp'

Roosevelt carrier group headed to sea

In a news conference at the Pentagon, Rumsfeld warned that the United States was in for a long fight against terrorist groups. He said the U.S. would go after terrorists by moving "to drain the swamp they live in."[81]

Trump continued the turn of phrase's tradition and has promised to reform term limits on members of Congress and restrict former executive branch bureaucrats from becoming lobbyists. This is clearly part of Trump's view that the government system in the US has become stagnant.

---

81   http://edition.cnn.com/2001/US/09/18/ret.defense.rumsfeld

Trump did not say this directly, but he certainly hinted at it during his inauguration speech, and then reiterated the point on Twitter and Facebook afterwards:

@realDonaldTrump 20 Jan 2017
Today we are not merely transferring power from one Administration to another, or from one party to another – but we are transferring...

@realDonaldTrump 20 Jan 2017
power from Washington, D.C. and giving it back to you, the American People. #InaugurationDay

At least, this is my interpretation of his intentions regarding government reform.

Having no previous public office experience, he is perfectly placed to push this idea as he can operate with impunity and without fear of cries of hypocrisy. This may even be the key to his political success, Trump represents the extreme change that people are looking for.

@realDonaldTrump 18 Oct 2016
I will Make Our Government Honest Again -- believe me. But first, I'm going to have to #DrainTheSwamp in DC. https://www.donaldjtrump.com/press-releases/ donald-j.-trumps-five-point-plan-for-ethics-reform ...

In a statement titled 'Donald J. Trump's five-point plan for ethics reform' issued on his website, Trump outlined his policy which focuses on stopping former executive branch officials from lobbying government as both domestic and representatives of foreign governments, as well as closing some funding loopholes that allow foreign lobbyists to raise money during elections. Part of Trump's campaign against Hillary Clinton and the Democrat Party centred on WikiLeaks pages that illustrated the Clintons were engaging in 'pay-to-play', which is exactly what Trump attributed to being part of the corruption in modern government.

The Atlantic

'She Created This Mess and She Knows It'

Why the WikiLeaks revelation about a "pay-to-play" deal with Morocco is a quintessential Clinton controversy.

The chief complaint that critics make about the Clinton Foundation is that the former and perhaps future presidents engaged in a "pay-to-play" scheme, whereby donors—many of them foreign governments—would contribute money to the charity in exchange for access to Bill or Hillary Clinton, or worse, beneficial treatment from the State Department.[82]

@realDonaldTrump 18 Oct 2016
Pay-to-play. Collusion. Cover-ups. And now bribery? So CROOKED. I will #DrainTheSwamp.

@realDonaldTrump 18 Oct 2016
It is time to #DrainTheSwamp **in Washington, D.C! Vote Nov. 8th to take down the** #RIGGED system!

@realDonaldTrump 18 Oct 2016
'Clinton Campaign Tried to Limit Damage From Classified Info on Email Server' #DrainTheSwamp

@realDonaldTrump 18 Oct 2016
Hillary is the most corrupt person to ever run for the presidency of the United States. #DrainTheSwamp

---

82 http://www.theatlantic.com/politics/archive/2016/10/hillary-clinton-foundation-morocco-wikileaks/505043

Throughout his #DrainTheSwamp campaign Trump made the Clintons the personification of the corruption he is trying to remove.

Yet his policies have a holistic quality, as in they are all interconnected. This holistic nugget could be highlighted in a number of places, regarding a number of policies. But it is entertaining to point it out here as reforming the executive branch to encourage growth and fresh approaches to new government has no direct links to the war on IS. Whereas former executive branch officials lobbying against the repeal of the ACA does have an effect on one of Trump's major campaign policies. It can be interpreted that 'drain the swamp' is merely a mechanism to allow Trump to push his administrative agenda without challenge.

 @realDonaldTrump 19 Oct 2016
I WILL DEFEAT ISIS. THEY HAVE BEEN AROUND TOO LONG! What has our leadership been doing? #DrainTheSwamp

 @realDonaldTrump 27 Oct 2016
Obamacare is a disaster. We must REPEAL & REPLACE. Tired of the lies, and want to #DrainTheSwamp? Get out & VOTE #TrumpPence16 & lets #MAGA!

 @realDonaldTrump 24 Oct 2016
We are winning and the press is refusing to report it. Don't let them fool you- get out and vote! #DrainTheSwamp **on November 8th!**

 @realDonaldTrump 24 Oct 2016
My contract with the American voter will restore honesty, accountability & CHANGE to Washington! #DrainTheSwamp

@realDonaldTrump 27 Oct 2016
I agree, @MMFlint- To all Americans, I see you & I hear you. I am your voice. Vote to #DrainTheSwamp w/ me on 11/8.

#BigLeagueTruth

@realDonaldTrump
We must bring the truth directly to hard-working Americans who want to take our country back. #BigLeagueTruth

In late September/early October 2016, in an assault against the mainstream media (MSM) and in reaction to MSM pointing out facts that Donald Trump got wrong during the Presidential debates, Trump launched #BigLeagueTruth and encouraged the everyday American to join the 'big league truth team'.

Washington Post

Fact-checking the first Clinton-Trump presidential debate

In the first debate between presidential contenders Donald Trump and Hillary Clinton, Trump repeatedly relied on troublesome and false facts that have been debunked throughout the campaign. Clinton stretched the truth on occasion, such as when she tried to wiggle out of her 2012 praise of the Trans Pacific Partnership as a "gold standard." But her misstatements paled in comparison to the list of Trump's exaggerations and falsehoods.[83]

---

83 https://www.washingtonpost.com/news/fact-checker/wp/2016/09/27/fact-checking-the-first-clinton-trump-presidential-debate/?utm_term=.435e8bb14d71

DonaldJTrump.com

We cannot count on the rigged MSM to bring the truth to the American people.

I need you to help me speak directly to the hard-working Americans who want to take our country back.

Join the Big League Truth Team and help fact check Crooked Hillary LIVE during the debates.[84]

Trump used the Vice President debate as the launch platform for his #BigLeagueTruth mechanism:

@TeamTrump

@timkaine has a pay-to-play problem just like Crooked @HillaryClinton #VPDebates #BigLeagueTruth

@realDonaldTrump

Sanctions Relief From Clinton-Obama Iran Nuclear Deal Likely Go to Terrorists: #BigLeagueTruth #VPDebate

Trump referenced an article published by CNN in January 2016:

CNN

John Kerry: Some sanctions relief money for Iran will go to terrorism

When asked about whether some of the $150 billion in sanctions relief to Iran would go to terrorist groups, Kerry reiterated that, after settling debts, Iran would receive closer to $55 billion. He conceded some of that could go to groups considered terrorists, saying there was nothing the U.S. could do to prevent that.

---

84   https://www.donaldjtrump.com/landing/rapid-response

"I think that some of it will end up in the hands of the IRGC or other entities, some of which are labeled terrorists," he said in the interview in Davos, referring to Iran's Revolutionary Guard Corps.

"You know, to some degree, I'm not going to sit here and tell you that every component of that can be prevented."

But he added that "right now, we are not seeing the early delivery of funds going to that kind of endeavor at this point in time."[85]

Looking at the volume of accusations of fake news and media bias that Trump tweeted, on volume alone, one could suggest that there is a smear campaign to discredit Donald Trump and that the 'big league truth' initiative is a way for him to inject some balance into the political reporting equation.

@realDonaldTrump 5 Jun 2016
I am watching @CNN very little lately because they are so biased against me. Shows are predictable garbage! CNN and MSM is one big lie!

The reality suggested that 'big league truth' is just another level of user (voter) engagement and a way for Trump to directly politically weaponise those supporters who signed up to the program.

@realDonaldTrump 19 Oct 2016
The 2nd Amendment is under siege. We need SCOTUS judges who will uphold the US Constitution. #Debate #BigLeagueTruth

---

85   http://edition.cnn.com/2016/01/21/politics/john-kerry-money-iran-sanctions-terrorism

@realDonaldTrump 9 Oct 2016
It's this simple. "Make America Great Again."
#debate #BigLeagueTruth

@realDonaldTrump 9 Oct 2016
I'm not proud of my locker room talk. But this world has serious problems. We need serious leaders.
#debate #BigLeagueTruth

@TeamTrump 9 Oct 2016
It's US vs. them! @realDonaldTrump will fight for you!
#BigLeagueTruth #Debates

The power behind social media is that it can be simply distilled down to 'just a conversation'. One could say that Trump acted hypocritically by doing what he accused mainstream media of doing, pushing his own agenda in the guise of hard facts. This is far from the case. Trump ran a social media election campaign, what he did with 'big league truth' was give his supporters a louder voice on social media, which meant more people were talking Trump, which was a good thing for the President Trump brand.

#MAGA

Make America Great Again was a phrase which really connected with the American psyche. Not only did it hint at Trump's patriotism but it contained a nostalgia, a romance. It harked back to an era when the American dream was achievable and an era when the US was an unchallenged world power. Today, the US is still a world power, there are just more countries staking a claim.

Hillary also had a strong campaign messages which included phrases such as 'forward together', 'I'm with her', and 'stronger together', yet these messages lack the aggression that makes 'Make America Great Again' such an empowering phrase.

First use

@realDonaldTrump 3 Mar 2016
"@blt21muttrades: People are just mad that you're doing so good so they are gonna do they're best to stop you. Not gonna happen #MAGA"

Although this was the first time he used it as an acronym, the phrase had been in Trump's lexicon for some time; during his candidacy speech, he used it twice.

The first time it was used to highlight the inability of current politicians:

> *'So I've watched the politicians. I've dealt with them all my life. If you can't make a good deal with a politician, then there's something wrong with you. You're certainly not very good. And that's what we have representing us. They will never make America great again. They don't even have a chance. They're controlled fully— they're controlled fully by the lobbyists, by the donors, and by the special interests, fully.'*

The second time it was used to stake his claim that he is the best thing for the American people:

> *'Sadly, the American dream is dead. But if I get elected president I will bring it back bigger and better and stronger than ever before, and we will make America great again.'*[86]

---

86   http://www.time.com/3923128/donald-trump-announcement-speech

@realDonaldTrump 27 Jul 2016
**Thank you to our amazing law enforcement officers!
#MAGA**

@realDonaldTrump 3 Aug 2016
**Thank you to the amazing law enforcement officers
today - in Daytona Beach, Florida! #LESM #MAGA**

@realDonaldTrump 20 Aug 2016
**We will bring America together as ONE country again
– united as Americans in common purpose and
common dreams. #MAGA**

@realDonaldTrump 15 Sep 2016
**Full transcript of economic plan - delivered
to the Economic Club of New York. #MAGA
https://www.facebook.com/DonaldTrump/
posts/10157698735525725:0 ...**

@realDonaldTrump 8 Oct 2016
**The media and establishment want me out of the race
so badly - I WILL NEVER DROP OUT OF THE RACE,
WILL NEVER LET MY SUPPORTERS DOWN! #MAGA**

@realDonaldTrump 19 Oct 2016
**One of my first acts as President will be to deport
the drug lords and then secure the border. #Debate
#MAGA**

Trump vs the world

During his campaign Trump insulted a number of countries around the world.

Mexico

@realDonaldTrump 12 Jul 2015
Mexico's biggest drug lord escapes from jail. Unbelievable corruption and USA is paying the price. I told you so!

The day before Trump's inauguration, 'El Chapo' is extradited to the US.

ABC News

El Chapo: Mexican drug lord Joaquin Guzman extradited to the United States

Notorious Mexican drug lord Joaquin "El Chapo" Guzman has been extradited from a prison in northern Mexico to the United States.

His lawyers had sought to block his extradition to the United States.

He said he did not think Mexico put "a whole lot of thought" into the timing of the extradition, that comes the day before Donald Trump's inauguration as US President, "but it certainly isn't a bad thing".[87]

As the article suggests, the timing of this extradition is… interesting.

---

87   http://www.abc.net.au/news/2017-01-20/mexican-drug-lord-el-chapo-extradited-to-the-us/8197168

@realDonaldTrump 13 Jul 2015
....likewise, billions of dollars gets brought into Mexico through the border. We get the killers, drugs & crime, they get the money!

China

@realDonaldTrump 17 May 2016
The pathetic new hit ad against me misrepresents the final line. "You can tell them to go BLANK themselves" - was about China, NOT WOMEN!

... and just in case you missed it the first time!

@realDonaldTrump 17 May 2016
Crooked Hillary Clinton put out an ad where I am misquoted on women. Can't believe she would misrepresent the facts! My hit was on China

Germany

@realDonaldTrump 6 Jan 2016
Germany is going through massive attacks to its people by the migrants allowed to enter the country. New Years Eve was a disaster. THINK!

@realDonaldTrump 9 Dec 2015
I told you @TIME Magazine would never pick me as person of the year despite being the big favorite They picked person who is ruining Germany

@realDonaldTrump 7 Jan 2016
Man shot inside Paris police station. Just announced that terror threat is at highest level. Germany is a total mess-big crime. GET SMART!

@realDonaldTrump 11 Jan 2017
Intelligence agencies should never have allowed this fake news to "leak" into the public. One last shot at me. Are we living in Nazi Germany?

Belgium

New York Times

Donald Trump Finds New City to Insult: Brussels

Asked by the Fox Business Network anchor Maria Bartiromo about the feasibility of his proposal to bar foreign Muslims from entering the United States, Mr. Trump argued that Belgium and France had been blighted by the failure of Muslims in these countries to integrate.

Warming to his theme, he added that Brussels was in a particularly dire state. "You go to Brussels — I was in Brussels a long time ago, 20 years ago, so beautiful, everything is so beautiful — it's like living in a hellhole right now," Mr. Trump continued.[88]

---

88   https://www.nytimes.com/2016/01/28/world/europe/trump-finds-new-city-to-insult-brussels.html?_r=0

@realDonaldTrump 24 Mar 2016
Remember when I recently said that Brussels is a "hell hole" and a mess and the failing @nytimes wrote a critical article. I was so right!

Saudi Arabia

@realDonaldTrump 29 Jun 2015
Saudi Arabia should be paying the United States many billions of dollars for our defense of them. Without us, gone!

@realDonaldTrump 12 Dec 2015
Dopey Prince @Alwaleed_Talal wants to control our U.S. politicians with daddy's money. Can't do it when I get elected. #Trump2016

@Alwaleed_Talal 11 Dec 2015
@realDonaldTrump **You are a disgrace not only to the GOP but to all America. Withdraw from the U.S presidential race as you will never win.**

November: Election month

Donald Trump began his end-game for the election on November 8. With only a week to go, Trump continued to push his 'make America great, Hillary Clinton is a crook and Obama, a.k.a. ObamaCare is rubbish' narrative.

@realDonaldTrump 2 Nov 2016
You can change your vote in six states. So, now that you see that Hillary was a big mistake, change your vote to MAKE AMERICA GREAT AGAIN!

@realDonaldTrump 2 Nov 2016
I am going to repeal and replace ObamaCare. We will have MUCH less expensive and MUCH better healthcare. With Hillary, costs will triple!

@realDonaldTrump 4 Nov 2016
If Obama worked as hard on straightening out our country as he has trying to protect and elect Hillary, we would all be much better off!

@realDonaldTrump 4 Nov 2016
The only thing that can stop this corrupt machine is YOU. The only force strong enough to save our country is US....

@realDonaldTrump 5 Nov 2016
MAKE AMERICA GREAT AGAIN!

@realDonaldTrump 7 Nov 2016
Our American comeback story begins 11/8/16. Together, we will MAKE AMERICA SAFE & GREAT again for everyone!

@realDonaldTrump 8 Nov 2016
TODAY WE MAKE AMERICA GREAT AGAIN!

Election day

Hillary Clinton won the popular vote (Trump 61,201,031 to Clinton 62,523,126), but Donald Trump came out on top in the all important electoral college vote (with 270 votes needed to win, Trump claimed 303 to Clinton's 232). Trump's victory speech lacked the aggression and hostility of his previous speeches:

> *'We must reclaim our country's destiny and dream big and bold and daring. We have to do that. We're going to dream of things for our country and beautiful things and successful things once again.*

> *'I want to tell the world community that while we will always put America's interests first, we will deal fairly with everyone, with everyone — all people and all other nations. We will seek common ground, not hostility; partnership, not conflict.'*[89]

The speech suggested Trump may have switched gears from combatant to diplomat, that the war campaign that he had been fighting against his political peers was just that, a war campaign executed on social media.

This sentiment lasted as long as his speech and within days the aggressive rhetoric that framed Trump through the campaign was back, however there had been a shift from a man fighting to win the support of his country to a man fighting to pursue his vision for his country. Unfortunately, his hostility extended to anyone, anywhere who stood in the way of the Trump presidential philosophy.

---

89 https://www.nytimes.com/2016/11/10/us/politics/trump-speech-transcript.html

Electoral aftermath

@realDonaldTrump 11 Nov 2016

A fantastic day in D.C. Met with President Obama for first time. Really good meeting, great chemistry. Melania liked Mrs. O a lot!

@realDonaldTrump 11 Nov 2016

Just had a very open and successful presidential election. Now professional protesters, incited by the media, are protesting. Very unfair!

New York Times
November 11, 2016

'Not Our President': Protests Spread After Donald Trump's Election

Thousands of people across the country marched, shut down highways, burned effigies and shouted angry slogans on Wednesday night to protest the election of Donald J. Trump as president.

The demonstrations, fuelled by social media, continued into the early hours of Thursday. The crowds swelled as the night went on but remained mostly peaceful.

Protests were reported in cities as diverse as Dallas and Oakland and included marches in Boston; Chicago; Portland, Ore.; Seattle and Washington and at college campuses in California, Massachusetts and Pennsylvania.[90]

After initially complaining, Trump quickly turned his rhetoric around and embraced the protests:

---

90   https://www.nytimes.com/2016/11/10/us/trump-election-protests.html

@realDonaldTrump 11 Nov 2016
Love the fact that the small groups of protesters last night have passion for our great country. We will all come together and be proud!

CNN
November 13

Anti-Trump protests move through fifth day

Protesters hit the streets Sunday over the election of Donald Trump, marking the fifth day of demonstrations in cities such as New York, Los Angeles and San Francisco.

In Manhattan, a group gathered to demonstrate against Trump's immigration policies.

"The main purpose is to tell Donald Trump he can't just deport 11 million undocumented people," Noelle Yasso said. "They're here to stay and we stand in solidarity with them."[91]

@realDonaldTrump 13 Nov 2016
The debates, especially the second and third, plus speeches and intensity of the large rallies, plus OUR GREAT SUPPORTERS, gave us the win!

Trump gets down to business

@realDonaldTrump 16 Nov 2016
Very organized process taking place as I decide on Cabinet and many other positions. I am the only one who knows who the finalists are!

---

91   http://edition.cnn.com/2016/11/13/us/protests-elections-trump

@realDonaldTrump 16 Nov 2016
The failing @nytimes story is so totally wrong on transition. It is going so smoothly. Also, I have spoken to many foreign leaders.

@realDonaldTrump 16 Nov 2016
I have received and taken calls from many foreign leaders despite what the failing @nytimes said. Russia, U.K., China, Saudi Arabia, Japan,

@realDonaldTrump 16 Nov 2016
Australia, New Zealand, and more. I am always available to them. @nytimes is just upset that they looked like fools in their coverage of me.

Recount scandal

The Guardian

Jill Stein requests Wisconsin recount, alleging hackers filed bogus absentee ballots

Jill Stein has requested a full recount of the presidential election in Wisconsin, alleging that foreign hackers could have skewed the result by obtaining the state's voter database and then filing bogus absentee ballots.

Stein, the Green party's candidate in the presidential election, formally filed for a recount with Wisconsin authorities shortly before the state's 5pm deadline on Friday. She also planned to request recounts in Michigan and Pennsylvania in the coming days.[92]

Trump was noticeably unimpressed by Jill Stein's action.

---

92 https://www.theguardian.com/us-news/2016/nov/25/jill-stein-election-recount-clinton-trump-michigan-pennsylvania-wisconsin

@realDonaldTrump 27 Nov 2016

The Green Party scam to fill up their coffers by asking for impossible recounts is now being joined by the badly defeated & demoralized Dems

The Guardian

Hillary Clinton urged to call for election vote recount in battleground states

A growing number of academics and activists are calling for US authorities to fully audit or recount the 2016 presidential election vote in key battleground states, in case the results could have been skewed by foreign hackers.

The loose coalition, which is urging Hillary Clinton's campaign to join its fight, is preparing to deliver a report detailing its concerns to congressional committee chairs and federal authorities early next week, according to two people involved.[93]

New York Times

Hillary Clinton's Team to Join Wisconsin Recount Pushed by Jill Stein

WASHINGTON — Nearly three weeks after Election Day, Hillary Clinton's campaign said on Saturday that it would participate in a recount process in Wisconsin incited by a third-party candidate and would join any potential recounts in two other closely contested states, Pennsylvania and Michigan.

---

93   https://www.theguardian.com/us-news/2016/nov/23/hillary-clinton-election-vote-recount-michigan-pennsylvania-wisconsin

The Clinton campaign held out little hope of success in any of the three states, and said it had seen no "actionable evidence" of vote hacking that might taint the results or otherwise provide new grounds for challenging Donald J. Trump's victory. But it suggested it was going along with the recount effort to assure supporters that it was doing everything possible to verify that hacking by Russia or other irregularities had not affected the results.[94]

Trump responded to the actions of Jill Stein and the Democrats in a string of ten tweets:

@realDonaldTrump 27 Nov 2016
The Democrats, when they incorrectly thought they were going to win, asked that the election night tabulation be accepted. Not so anymore!

@realDonaldTrump 27 Nov 2016
Hillary Clinton conceded the election when she called me just prior to the victory speech and after the results were in. Nothing will change

@realDonaldTrump 27 Nov 2016
Hillary's debate answer on delay: "That is horrifying. That is not the way our democracy works. Been around for 240 years. We've had free

@realDonaldTrump 27 Nov 2016
and fair elections. We've accepted the outcomes when we may not have liked them, and that is what must be expected of anyone standing on a

---

94   https://www.nytimes.com/2016/11/26/us/politics/clinton-camp-will-join-push-for-wisconsin-ballot-recount.html

@realDonaldTrump 27 Nov 2016
during a general election. I, for one, am appalled that somebody that is the nominee of one of our two major parties would take that kind

@realDonaldTrump 27 Nov 2016
of position." Then, separately she stated, "He said something truly horrifying ... he refused to say that he would respect the results of

@realDonaldTrump 27 Nov 2016
this election. That is a direct threat to our democracy." She then said, "We have to accept the results and look to the future, Donald

@realDonaldTrump 27 Nov 2016
Trump is going to be our President. We owe him an open mind and the chance to lead." So much time and money will be spent - same result! Sad

@realDonaldTrump 27 Nov 2016
It would have been much easier for me to win the so-called popular vote than the Electoral College in that I would only campaign in 3 or 4

@realDonaldTrump 27 Nov 2016
states instead of the 15 states that I visited. I would have won even more easily and convincingly (but smaller states are forgotten)!

@realDonaldTrump 28 Nov 2016
Serious voter fraud in Virginia, New Hampshire and California - so why isn't the media reporting on this? Serious bias - big problem!

Trump vs flag burners

One of the many anti-Trump protests that happened after the election was a student protest at a private college. As part of the protest, a US flag was burned.

New York Times

Hampshire College Draws Protests Over Removal of U.S. Flag

A group of military veterans protested at a private Massachusetts college over the weekend, objecting to a decision by the college to allow the American flag to be removed from its main flagpole, and adding their voices to a debate on a campus that has seen the flag lowered, removed and even burned since the election.

Some on campus perceived the flag as "a powerful symbol of fear they've felt all their lives because they grew up in marginalized communities, never feeling safe," the college's president, Jonathan Lash, said in a statement.[95]

Nobody is quite sure what prompted Trump to tweet, possibly the report of the protest, which included the detail of the flag being burnt.

@realDonaldTrump 29 Nov 2016

Nobody should be allowed to burn the American flag - if they do, there must be consequences - perhaps loss of citizenship or year in jail!

As random as his tweet seemed, the public reaction to Trump's tweet was strong. In the US, flag burning is allowed under

---

95   https://www.nytimes.com/2016/11/28/us/hampshire-college-flag-veterans-protest.html

the first amendment as it is considered a form of freedom of speech. Constitutional rights frequently come up in American politics; Trump frequently urged his supporters to fight against changes to the Second amendment during his campaign.

@realDonaldTrump 2 Jul 2016

The #2A to our Constitution is clear. The right of the people to keep & bear Arms shall not be infringed upon.

To argue that it is every American's constitutional right to own a gun but that it should be deemed illegal, very illegal, to assert every American's constitutional right to practice freedom of speech and burn the flag is hypocritical. This may be merely part of a bigger narrative that might reveal itself over the next four years, a narrative where the American dream can only be revitalised through strict police enforcement of certain acts (including immigration law). But this is merely speculation and this book tries to avoid drawing assumptions and speculating about the future.

Trump's naughty list

Donald Trump was a Presidential candidate that wore his heart on his sleeve; love you or hate you, if he had an opinion about you he was likely to express it. As with all things controversial, the naughty list is much more fun than the nice list. Journalists, politicians, commentators, celebrities, authors — beware, if you make it onto Trump's naughty list, he is likely to tell the world through Twitter. Some of Trump's naughty list tweets have obvious roots, some do not. An explanation for why a person made the naughty list has been added, where necessary.

The New York Times

@realDonaldTrump 2 Jul 2016
Just read in the failing @nytimes that I was not aware "the event had to be held in Cleveland" - a total lie. These people are sick!

One could write an entire book on Trump's war with the media during his campaign, but he seemed to dedicate an entire war front to the *New York Times*. The paper's roots may be conservative but they haven't favoured a Republican candidate since 1956, suggesting a swing to the left. The important point to note is that the behaviour of the *New York Times* during the election campaign is not out of character. The paper addressed the question in a column published in July 2016.

New York Times Public Editor Column

Like the tiresome bore at a party, I went around asking several journalists in the newsroom about these claims that The Times sways to the left. Mostly I was met with a roll of the eyes. All sides hate us, they said. We're tough on everyone. That's nothing new here.

It's part of a fracturing media environment that reflects a fractured country.[96]

John King

@realDonaldTrump 10 Jul 2016
I heard that the underachieving John King of @CNN on Inside Politics was one hour of lies. Happily, few people are watching - dead network!

Supreme Court Justice Ruth Ginsberg

@realDonaldTrump 13 Jul 2016
Justice Ginsburg of the U.S. Supreme Court has embarrassed all by making very dumb political statements about me. Her mind is shot - resign!

CNN

Justice Ruth Bader Ginsburg calls Trump a 'faker,' he says she should resign

Supreme Court Justice Ruth Ginsberg called Trump a faker and said that he lacked consistency.[97]

---

96   https://www.nytimes.com/2016/07/24/public-editor/liz-spayd-the-new-york-times-public-editor.html

97   http://edition.cnn.com/2016/07/12/politics/justice-ruth-bader-ginsburg-donald-trump-faker

Democrat Senator Elizabeth Warren

@realDonaldTrump 17 Jul 2016
Goofy Elizabeth Warren, who may be the least productive Senator in the U.S. Senate, must prove she is not a fraud. Without the con it's over

Democrat Senator Elizabeth Warren and Trump have a history of lashing out at each other. Warren gave as good as she got and fought fire with fire.

Elizabeth Warren Facebook post
March 2016

Let's be honest – Donald Trump is a loser.

More than anyone we've seen before come within reach of the presidency, Donald Trump stands ready to tear apart an America that was built on values like decency, community, and concern for our neighbors. Many of history's worst authoritarians started out as losers – and Trump is a serious threat. The way I see it, it's our job to make sure he ends this campaign every bit the loser that he started it.[98]

Elizabeth Warren reacted to Trump allegedly inciting a pro-2A crowd to shoot Hillary Clinton with the following tweets:

@elizabethforma 9 Aug 2016
@realDonaldTrump **makes death threats because he's a pathetic coward who can't handle the fact that he's losing to a girl.**

---

98   https://www.facebook.com/ElizabethWarren/posts/10153621490203687

@elizabethforma 9 Aug 2016
**Your reckless comments sound like a two-bit dictator,
@realDonaldTrump Not a man who wants to lead the
greatest democracy on the planet.**

Governor of Ohio, John Kasich

@realDonaldTrump 20 Jul 2016
**John Kasich was never asked by me to be V.P. Just
arrived in Cleveland - will be a great two days!**

Donald Trump and the Governor of Ohio, John Kasich go to
war in the media over claims that Trump wanted Kasich to be
his VP running mate. Kasich insisted that Trump was going to
make him an offer and Trump insisted that this was never
the case.

Republican Senator Ted Cruz

@realDonaldTrump 21 Jul 2016
**Wow, Ted Cruz got booed off the stage, didn't honour
the pledge! I saw his speech two hours early but let
him speak anyway. No big deal!**

In a twist that mirrors Trump's stance at the start of the
Republican debates, Cruz is unable to honour his pledge to
support Trump during the GOP convention.

Former Mayor of New York Michael Bloomberg

@realDonaldTrump 29 Jul 2016
**"Little" Michael Bloomberg, who never had the guts
to run for president, knows nothing about me. His last
term as Mayor was a disaster!**

During the Democratic National Convention, former New York City mayor and now billionaire, Bloomberg urged independents to vote for Hillary.

Khizr Khan

@realDonaldTrump 1 Aug 2016
Mr. Khan, who does not know me, viciously attacked me from the stage of the DNC and is now all over T.V. doing the same - Nice!

Barack Obama

@realDonaldTrump 2 Aug 2016
President Obama will go down as perhaps the worst president in the history of the United States!

At the height of the August Trump/Obama fight, Trump tweeted in retaliation to President Obama publicly announcing, in front of another country's leader, that Trump was unfit for the presidency.

Michael Morell

@realDonaldTrump 7 Aug 2016
Michael Morell, the lightweight former Acting Director of C.I.A., and a man who has made serious bad calls, is a total Clinton flunky!

A reaction to Michael Morell siding with Hillary Clinton.

Hosts on **MSNBC**

@realDonaldTrump 2 Sep 2016
Just heard that crazy and very dumb @morningmika
had a mental breakdown while talking about me on
the low ratings @Morning_Joe. Joe a mess!

Television personalities @morningmika and @Morning_Joe
are talent on the MSNBC news network.

CNN

@realDonaldTrump 3 Sep 2016
@CNN is so disgusting in their bias, but they are having
a hard time promoting Crooked Hillary in light of the
new e-mail scandals.

Jeff Flake

@realDonaldTrump 4 Sep 2016
The Republican Party needs strong and committed
leaders, not weak people such as @JeffFlake, if it is
going to stop illegal immigration.

Tony Schwartz: The art of the deal

@realDonaldTrump 10 Sep 2016
Dummy writer @tonyschwartz, who wanted to do a
second book with me for years (I said no), is now a
hostile basket case who feels jilted!

@realDonaldTrump 10 Sep 2016
I haven't seen @tonyschwartz in many years, he hardly knows me. Never liked his style. Super lib, Crooked H supporter. Irrelevant dope!

Mr Schwartz co-wrote *The Art of the Deal* in the late 1980s. Trump's tweets were due to Schwartz stating that he thought Trump was an unsuitable candidate for the presidency.

Colin Powell

@realDonaldTrump 15 Sep 2016
I was never a fan of Colin Powell after his weak understanding of weapons of mass destruction in Iraq = disaster. We can do much better!

ABC

Colin Powell accuses Hillary Clinton of hubris, blasts Donald Trump as 'national disgrace': leaked emails [99]

Defence Secretary Robert Gates

@realDonaldTrump 17 Sep 2016
I never met former Defence Secretary Robert Gates. He knows nothing about me. But look at the results under his guidance - a total disaster!

Another person who thinks Trump is unsuitable to be President.

---

99   http://www.abc.net.au/news/2016-09-15/us-election-email-leak/7846290

The press's right to use anonymous sources

@realDonaldTrump 30 Sep 2016
Anytime you see a story about me or my campaign saying "sources said," DO NOT believe it. There are no sources, they are just made up lies!

This one would probably be attributed to 'anyone who quotes something negative about me and does not name the source'.

The Staten Island media group (SILive.com) published an article reminding their readers of their first amendment rights.

> "The media depend to a large extent on members of the public for the supply of information of public interest. Most of the time, these sources are more than happy to be quoted in the newspaper or on the television. But occasionally, citizens come forward with information of a secret or highly sensitive nature," says Article 19.

> "Anonymity is often a precondition for the source's willingness to speak, out of fear for retaliation if his or her name were made public," adds Article 19. [100]

The Republican Party

In the wake of the 2005 recording of Trump's misogynistic approach to women, large swathes of the Republican Party distanced themselves from Trump in a pre-emptive move, in case the Republican Party needed to replace Trump. Paul Ryan, Speaker of the House of Representatives, was one of many who spoke out against Trump.

---

100 http://www.silive.com/news/index.ssf/2016/09/what_did_trump_say_in_his_morn.html

@realDonaldTrump 9 Oct 2016
So many self-righteous hypocrites. Watch their poll numbers – and elections – go down!

@realDonaldTrump 11 Oct 2016
Despite winning the second debate in a landslide (every poll), it is hard to do well when Paul Ryan and others give zero support!

The Foreign Office

Trump named and shamed the Foreign Office for talking about planned military action overseas. Trump would prefer if the fight against terrorism was not reported publicly.

@realDonaldTrump 11 Oct 2016
The very foul mouthed Sen. John McCain begged for my support during his primary (I gave, he won), then dropped me over locker room remarks!

@realDonaldTrump 11 Oct 2016
The attack on Mosul is turning out to be a total disaster. We gave them months of notice. U.S. is looking so dumb. VOTE TRUMP and WIN AGAIN!

Social Media

@realDonaldTrump 30 Oct 2016
Wow, Twitter, Google and Facebook are burying the FBI criminal investigation of Clinton. Very dishonest media!

Chuck Jones

@realDonaldTrump 8 Dec 2016
Chuck Jones, who is President of United Steelworkers 1999, has done a terrible job representing workers. No wonder companies flee country!

The Washington Post reported that Chuck Jones, leader of the Steelworkers union criticised Trump for not acting on his plan to keep manufacturing in the US:

Washington Post

Chuck Jones speaks badly of Trump. Carrier are closing down and moving to Mexico, Chuck has a situation where lots of his Union members are going to lose their jobs.

'I represent the Carrier Workers whose jobs Donald Trump has pledged to save. And I'm tired of being lied to.' [101]

NBC

@realDonaldTrump 12 Dec 2016
Just watched @NBCNightlyNews - So biased, inaccurate and bad, point after point. Just can't get much worse, although @CNN is right up there!

Graydon Carter and Vanity Fair

@realDonaldTrump 26 Dec 2016
Has anyone looked at the really poor numbers of @VanityFair Magazine. Way down, big trouble, dead! Graydon Carter, no talent, will be out!

---

101   https://www.washingtonpost.com/posteverything/wp/2016/12/08/im-the-union-leader-donald-trump-attacked-im-tired-of-being-lied-to-about-our-jobs/?utm_term=.0cb59f77ce7c

The U.N.

@realDonaldTrump 26 Dec 2016
The United Nations has such great potential but right now it is just a club for people to get together, talk and have a good time. So sad!

Trump and Israel vs the US and the United Nations.
The UN Security council voted to condemn a number of Israeli settlements in Jerusalem and the West Bank, the US abstained from voting on this politically hot topic. Through tweets and political stances, Trump has established that he is very pro-Israel.[102]

@realDonaldTrump 22 Sep 2015
Yom Kippur blessings to all of my friends in Israel and around the world. #YomKippur

@realDonaldTrump 13 Jul 2016
Is President Obama trying to destroy Israel with all his bad moves? Think about it and let me know!

@realDonaldTrump 13 Jul 2016
The Republican platform is most pro-Israel of all time!

@realDonaldTrump 28 Dec 2016
We cannot continue to let Israel be treated with such total disdain and disrespect. They used to have a great friend in the U.S., but.......

---

102 http://www.news.com.au/finance/work/leaders/donald-trump-says-united-nations-is-just-a-club-for-people-to-have-a-good-time/news-story/04c626e485d7404144bbac95dc05d28b

@realDonaldTrump 28 Dec 2016

not anymore. The beginning of the end was the horrible Iran deal, and now this (U.N.)! Stay strong Israel, January 20th is fast approaching!

Toyota

@realDonaldTrump 5 Jan 2017

Toyota Motor said will build a new plant in Baja, Mexico, to build Corolla cars for U.S. NO WAY! Build plant in U.S. or pay big border tax

Arnold Schwarzenegger

Trump tried to terminate the terminator by taking a dig at Arnold Schwarzenegger as his replacement on *Celebrity Apprentice*.[103]

@realDonaldTrump 6 Jan 2017

Wow, the ratings are in and Arnold Schwarzenegger got "swamped" (or destroyed) by comparison to the ratings machine, DJT. So much for....

@realDonaldTrump 6 Jan 2017

being a movie star-and that was season 1 compared to season 14. Now compare him to my season 1. But who cares, he supported Kasich & Hillary

What makes this pop at Arnold Schwarzenegger so interesting is that in December 2016 CNN reported that Donald Trump planned to do *The Apprentice* whilst serving as President, something which Trump immediately shot down as fake news.

---

103 http://www.news.com.au/entertainment/tv/reality-tv/donald-trump-slams-celebrity-apprentice-host-arnold-schwarzenegger/news-story/72044071300d96 5e4acc0ee82e568ea9

@realDonaldTrump 10 Dec 2016

Reports by @CNN that I will be working on The Apprentice during my Presidency, even part time, are ridiculous & untrue - FAKE NEWS!

Which begs the question to be asked, if Donald Trump has severed all connections to *The Apprentice*, why does he care so much about the ratings?

John Lewis

Civil rights activist and Democrat John Lewis commented that Trump was not a legitimate candidate. In what one must assume was an attempt to discredit a popular political figure, Trump discredited him on Twitter. The public reaction rocketed Lewis's books on the US Civil Rights movement up the bestseller list.[104]

@realDonaldTrump 14 Jan 2017

Congressman John Lewis should spend more time on fixing and helping his district, which is in horrible shape and falling apart (not to......

@realDonaldTrump 14 Jan 2017

mention crime infested) rather than falsely complaining about the election results. All talk, talk, talk - no action or results. Sad!

---

104 https://www.theguardian.com/books/2017/jan/16/john-lewis-clash-with-donald-trump-sends-the-civil-rights-heros-book-to-no-1

10 things Donald Trump thinks are sad

In what looked like the poorly executed use of American slang — because if it only means 'unhappy' then I would hate to see Trump angry at the Iran deal — Trump has commented on his political peers throughout his campaign. Here are 10 of the best.

@realDonaldTrump 22 Aug 2015
How is Bernie Sanders going to defend our country if he can't even defend his own microphone? Very sad!

@realDonaldTrump 9 Sep 2015
See you in D.C. tomorrow at 1:00 P.M. at the Capitol to protest the horribly negotiated deal with Iran. Really sad!

@realDonaldTrump 28 Oct 2015
Does anybody think that @CNBC will get their fictitious polling numbers corrected sometime prior to the start of the debate. Sad!

@realDonaldTrump 20 Dec 2015
Hillary Clinton spokesperson admitted that their was no ISIS video of me. Therefore, Hillary LIED at the debate last night. SAD!

@realDonaldTrump 23 Jan 2016
The only reason irrelevant @GlennBeck doesn't like me is I refused to do his failing show - asked many times. Very few listeners - sad!

@realDonaldTrump 3 Mar 2016
Because of me, the Republican Party has taken in millions of new voters, a record. If they are not careful, they will all leave. Sad!

@realDonaldTrump 20 Mar 2016
Why is it that the horrendous protesters, who scream, curse punch, shut down roads/doors during my **RALLIES**, are never blamed by media? SAD!

@realDonaldTrump 24 Mar 2016
Europe and the U.S. must immediately stop taking in people from Syria. This will be the destruction of civilization as we know it! So sad!

@realDonaldTrump 4 May 2016
Wow, Lyin' Ted Cruz really went wacko today. Made all sorts of crazy charges. Can't function under pressure - not very presidential. Sad!

@realDonaldTrump 13 Jul 2016
Despite spending $500k a day on TV ads alone #CrookedHillary falls flat in nationwide @QuinnipiacPoll. Having ZERO impact. Sad!!

December:
Presidential business

Trump's plan to energise the US economy is focused on encouraging businesses that cater to US customers to manufacture their goods in the US. During his victory lap in the second half of November, Trump tweeted his approval of several businesses that had announced they were keeping their factories domestic.

@realDonaldTrump 18 Nov 2016
Just got a call from my friend Bill Ford, Chairman of Ford, who advised me that he will be keeping the Lincoln plant in Kentucky - no Mexico

@realDonaldTrump 18 Nov 2016
I worked hard with Bill Ford to keep the Lincoln plant in Kentucky. I owed it to the great State of Kentucky for their confidence in me!

@realDonaldTrump 24 Nov 2016
I am working hard, even on Thanksgiving, trying to get Carrier A.C. Company to stay in the U.S. (Indiana). MAKING PROGRESS - Will know soon!

@realDonaldTrump 30 Nov 2016
Big day on Thursday for Indiana and the great workers of that wonderful state. We will keep our companies and jobs in the U.S. Thanks Carrier

In stark contrast to this, during the first week of December, Trump tweeted that Rexnord, who manufacture engine components, were NOT keeping their operation domestic.

@realDonaldTrump 3 Dec 2016
Rexnord of Indiana is moving to Mexico and rather viciously firing all of its 300 workers. This is happening all over our country. No more!

What followed was President-elect Donald Trump's six tweet plan (although it could be interpreted as a threat) to encourage businesses to manufacture domestically by punishing them with inflated import taxation.

@realDonaldTrump 4 Dec 2016
The U.S. is going to substantially reduce taxes and regulations on businesses, but any business that leaves our country for another country

@realDonaldTrump 4 Dec 2016
fires its employees, builds a new factory or plant in the other country, and then thinks it will sell its product back into the U.S. ...

@realDonaldTrump 4 Dec 2016
without retribution or consequence, is WRONG! There will be a tax on our soon to be strong border of 35% for these companies...

@realDonaldTrump 4 Dec 2016
wanting to sell their product, cars, A.C. units etc., back across the border. This tax will make leaving financially difficult, but...

@realDonaldTrump 4 Dec 2016
these companies are able to move between all 50 states, with no tax or tariff being charged. Please be forewarned prior to making a very ...

@realDonaldTrump 4 Dec 2016

expensive mistake! THE UNITED STATES IS OPEN FOR BUSINESS

@realDonaldTrump 29 Dec 2016

2017: Happy New Year from the President-elect!

@realDonaldTrump 31 Dec 2016
Happy New Year to all, including to my many enemies and those who have fought me and lost so badly they just don't know what to do. Love!

At the time of tweeting, Donald Trump was weeks away from becoming the leader of one of the most powerful and influential nations on Earth. The language is what we are used to hearing from Trump and his message is consistent with similar tweets from previous years.

His 2015 message was unusually positive but Trump was building up to an election campaign.

@realDonaldTrump 31 Dec 2015
HAPPY NEW YEAR & THANK YOU!

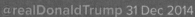

@realDonaldTrump 31 Dec 2014
To EVERYONE, including all haters and losers, HAPPY NEW YEAR. Work hard, be smart and always remember, WINNING TAKES CARE OF EVERYTHING!

@realDonaldTrump 31 Dec 2013
Make sure to have fun and celebrate NYE with friends and family. Happy New Year everyone!

@realDonaldTrump 24 Dec 2013
I'd like to wish all of my friends--and even my many enemies--a very Merry Christmas and Happy New Year.

The shocking aspect of Trump's 2016/17 message is that his tweet read like a taunt, a brag. It felt like he was saying to the world, but specifically his political, commercial, and now geographical enemies, 'I am unstoppable, live with it'.

This may be behaviour consistent with a successful and aggressively active businessman but is not necessarily the behaviour people expect from the leader of the United States in modern times. Twitter users responded well.

@Samir_Madani 31 Dec 2016
@realDonaldTrump **If folks report his account for abusive trolling, do you think Twitter will ban him? Asking for a friend. Happy New Year!**

@ShellHawk Jan 1
@Samir_Madani **Definitely against their Terms & Conditions. We should report it, at least so WWIII won't be launched with a fucking Tweet!**

Trump vs celebrity

At the 2017 Golden Globe Awards on January 8, Meryl Streep used her acceptance speech for a lifetime achievement award as a political platform. Key parts of her speech, which was an obvious 'call-out' to Trump, included:

> *You and all of us in this room, really, belong to the most vilified segments in American society right now. Think about it. Hollywood, foreigners, and the press.*

> *There was one performance this year that stunned me. It sank its hooks in my heart. Not because it was good. There was nothing good about it. But it was effective and it did its job. It made its intended audience laugh and show their teeth. It was that moment when the person asking to sit in the most respected seat in our country imitated a disabled reporter, someone he outranked in privilege, power, and the capacity to fight back. It kind of broke my heart when I saw it. I still can't get it out of my head because it wasn't in a movie. It was real life.*

> *Disrespect invites disrespect. Violence incites violence. When the powerful use their position to bully others, we all lose.*

Trump lashed out at Meryl Streep on Twitter. The general surprise and media (both mainstream and social) buzz generated was more a reaction to his imminent inauguration than his characteristically consistent response to criticism.

@realDonaldTrump Jan 9 2017
Meryl Streep, one of the most over-rated actresses in Hollywood, doesn't know me but attacked last night at the Golden Globes. She is a...

@realDonaldTrump Jan 9 2017
Hillary flunky who lost big. For the 100th time, I never "mocked" a disabled reporter (would never do that) but simply showed him...

@realDonaldTrump Jan 9 2017
"groveling" when he totally changed a 16 year old story that he had written in order to make me look bad. Just more very dishonest media!

With just 11 days to go until Donald Trump became one of the most powerful people in the world, the Twitterverse came up with a gem of a Trump-trolling hashtag: #ThingsTrumpThinkAreOverated.

@Inucroft 11 Jan 2017
@realDonaldTrump
#ThingsTrumpThinkAreOverrated
Facts
Human sufffering
Sanity
Human life
Common sense
Mental Disability
Physical Disability

@Jennie30041 11 Jan 2017
A Filter.
Restraint.
#ThingsTrumpThinkAreOverrated

> @simonizer888 11 Jan 2017
> Canada. Free Trade. Immigration. Mexico. Diversity.
> Tolerance. Life. Liberty. The Pursuit of Happiness.
> #ThingsTrumpThinkAreOverrated

Meryl Streep is not the first celebrity to mock, and be mocked by, Donald Trump on his path to the Oval Office. Alec Baldwin appeared in a number of *Saturday Night Live* (*SNL*) sketches in the guise of 'President Trump'.

> @realDonaldTrump 16 Oct 2016
> Watched Saturday Night Live hit job on me. Time to retire the boring and unfunny show. Alec Baldwin portrayal stinks. Media rigging election!

Saturday Night Live has a history of performing political skits that poke fun at the top tier of US government. Hillary Clinton, George W. Bush, Sarah Palin and Barack Obama have all been targets of *SNL*'s comedy.

In November 2015, while campaigning for the Republican nomination, Trump appeared on *Saturday Night Live* in person.

> @realDonaldTrump 9 Nov 2015
> Thank you to all of those who gave me such wonderful reviews for my performance on @nbcsnl Saturday Night Live. Best ratings in 4 years!

Alec Baldwin's impersonation of President Trump proved popular and it seemed the more Trump complained the more Alec Baldwin was compelled to troll him on Twitter to get a rise.

> @realDonaldTrump 20 Nov 2016
> I watched parts of @nbcsnl Saturday Night Live last night. It is a totally one-sided, biased show - nothing funny at all. Equal time for us?

@ABFalecbaldwin 20 Nov 2016
@realDonaldTrump Equal time? Election is over.
There is no more equal time. Now u try 2 b Pres +
ppl respond. That's pretty much it.

(@ABFoundation (Alec Baldwin Foundation) is the
charitable vehicle set up by Alec Baldwin to allow
him to do charitable work.)

@realDonaldTrump 4 Dec 2016
Just tried watching Saturday Night Live - unwatchable!
Totally biased, not funny and the Baldwin
impersonation just can't get any worse. Sad

Huffington Post
January 7, 2017

Alec Baldwin Trolls Donald Trump With A Russian 'Make America Great Again'

He's able to do an uncannily good impression of the US president-elect — but now Alec Baldwin has taken his trolling a step further.

The actor posted a selfie of him wearing Donald Trump's signature "Make America Great Again" hat.

But this version had a Russian twist.[105]

On February 11, 2017, Alec Baldwin hosted *Saturday Night Live*. The show contained a bumper bundle of Trump sketches.

---

105 http://www.huffingtonpost.co.uk/entry/alex-baldwin-trolls-donald-trump-with-a-russian-make-america-great-again_uk_587112e8e4b0cf4ed40eb000

On January 14, 2017, Mark Hamill, of *Star Wars* fame and who voices 'The Joker' in a lot of the Batman animated series and video games, published on Twitter a series of audio clips of him reading the tweets of Donald Trump in the voice of 'The Joker'.

> **@HamillHimself** 14 Jan 2017
> **Am I the ONLY one man enough to confront this** #OverratedFlunkyLoser **without resorting to an ad hominem assault?** https://audioboom.com/boos/5495377

As 'The Joker', Mark Hamil has read Donald Trump's happy new year tweet, as well as the three-tweet rant about Meryl Streep. He used the hashtag #Trumpster for his Joker/Trump commentary.

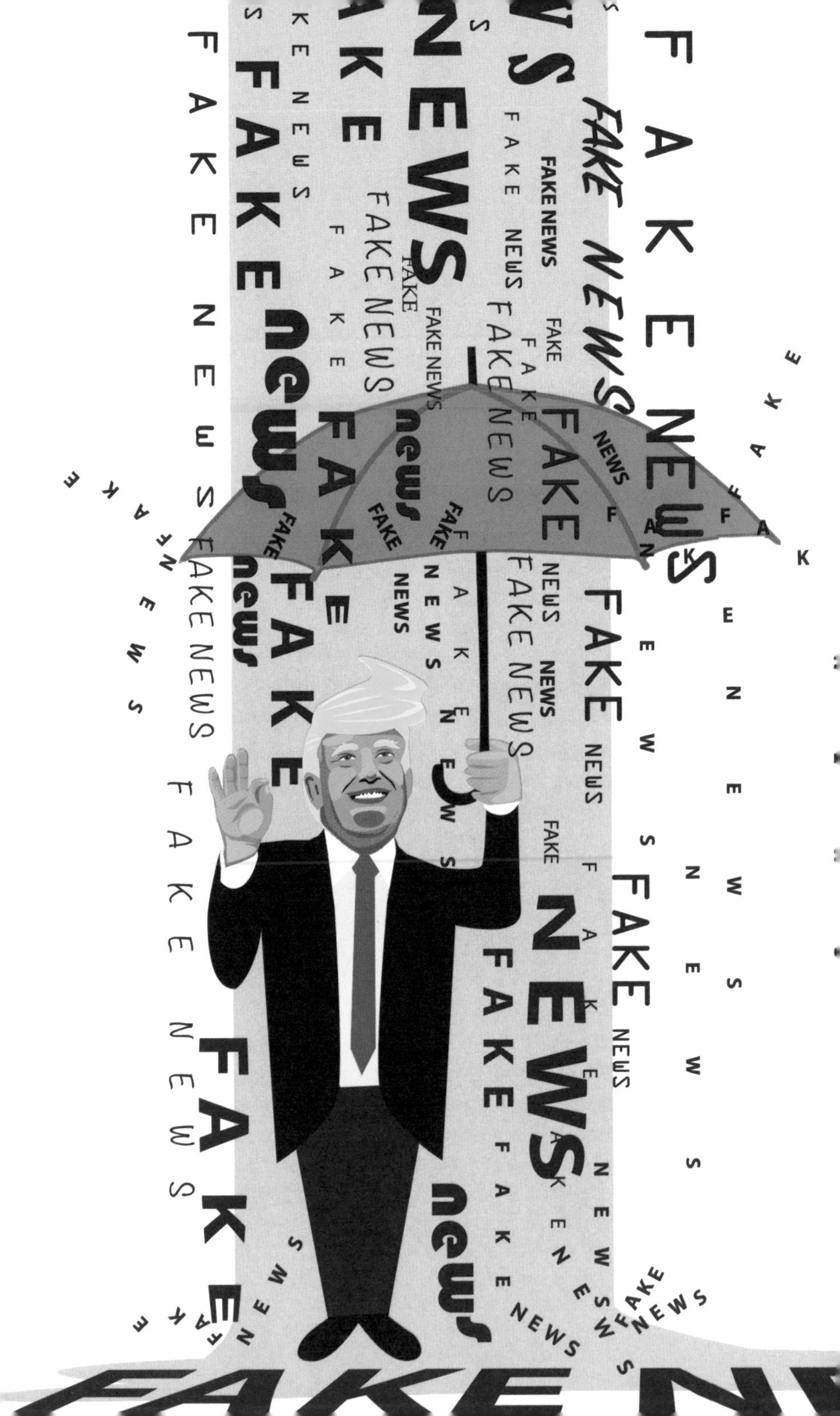
FAKE NEWS
FAKE NEWS
FAKE NEWS
FAKE NEWS
FAKE NEWS
FAKE NEWS

Trump and the #dishonest #failing #FAKE NEWS fray

@realDonaldTrump 5 Dec 2016

If the press would cover me accurately & honourably, I would have far less reason to "tweet." Sadly, I don't know if that will ever happen!

We have established that Trump used social media, especially Twitter, as a vehicle of retaliation against anyone who disagreed with him. When it comes to news agencies and journalists within those agencies, he used a number of buzzword labels: dishonest, failing and FAKE NEWS (it is almost always in capitals).

@realDonaldTrump 24 Sep 2015

The failing @politico news outlet, which I hear is losing lots of money, is really dishonest!

@realDonaldTrump 9 Dec 2015

The failing @nytimes does not mention the new @CNN Poll that has me leading Iowa by a massive 13 points – I am at 33%. Maggie Haberman, sad!

@realDonaldTrump 24 Dec 2015

Third rate reporters Amy Chozick and Maggie Haberman of the failing @nytimes are totally in the Hillary circle of bias. Think about Bill!

@realDonaldTrump 28 May 2016

I am always on the front page of the failing @nytimes, but when I won the GOP nomination, I'm in the back of the paper. Very dishonest!

@realDonaldTrump 15 Oct 2016
The failing @nytimes reporters don't even call us anymore, they just write whatever they want to write, making up sources along the way!

It is clear that Trump seriously disagreed with the way in which the *New York Times* reported news. Previously we looked at Donald Trump's campaign against CNN, but other networks come under fire from Trump too, even Fox News. Note that although he was clearly irritated by Fox News's stance, he did not use any of his usual buzzwords.

@realDonaldTrump 7 Aug 2015
I really enjoyed the debate tonight even though the @FoxNews trio, especially @megynkelly, was not very good or professional!

@realDonaldTrump 9 Aug 2015
It amazes me that other networks seem to treat me so much better than @FoxNews. I brought them the biggest ratings in history, & I get zip!

@realDonaldTrump 22 Sep 2015
@oreillyfactor was very negative to me in refusing to post the great polls that came out today including NBC. @FoxNews not good for me!

@realDonaldTrump 23 Sep 2015
@FoxNews has been treating me very unfairly & I have therefore decided that I won't be doing any more Fox shows for the foreseeable future.

Donald Trump's falling out with Fox News happened very early in his campaign. By the time his election campaign was in full swing, Fox News was back on side.

@realDonaldTrump 24 Jul 2016
The @CNN panels are so one sided, almost all against Trump. @FoxNews is so much better and the ratings are much higher. Don't watch CNN!

Trump didn't just focus on specific networks; at times Trump used blanket terms and accused mainstream media (MSM) of being against him. In December 2015, during a speech, Donald Trump commented on how Hillary Clinton got 'schlonged' by Barack Obama during the 2008 election.

The Independent

"Donald Trump says Hillary Clinton was 'schlonged' to presidency by Barack Obama"[106]

Washington Post

Donald Trump's 'schlonged': A linguistic investigation[107]

CNN

Donald Trump: Hillary Clinton 'got schlonged' in 2008[108]

All dictionary definitions of schlong and schlonged refer to a penis or the act of being hit in the face by a penis, Trump disagreed.

---

106 http://www.independent.co.uk/news/world/americas/us-elections/donald-trump-says-hillary-clinton-was-schlonged-to-the-presidency-by-barack-obama-a6782536.html

107 https://www.washingtonpost.com/news/morning-mix/wp/2015/12/22/donald-trumps-schlonged-a-linguistic-investigation/?utm_term=.c968ba056e92

108 http://edition.cnn.com/2015/12/21/politics/donald-trump-hillary-clinton-disgusting

@realDonaldTrump 23 Dec 2015

Once again, #MSM is dishonest. "Schlonged" is not vulgar. When I said Hillary got "schlonged" that meant beaten badly.

A year later, Trump was still picking holes in the media's coverage of his campaign.

@realDonaldTrump 6 Sep 2016

Mainstream media never covered Hillary's massive "hacking" or coughing attack, yet it is #1 trending. What's up?

@realDonaldTrump 12 Oct 2016

Very little pick-up by the dishonest media of incredible information provided by WikiLeaks. So dishonest! Rigged system!

@realDonaldTrump 10 Dec 2016

Reports by @CNN that I will be working on The Apprentice during my Presidency, even part time, are ridiculous & untrue - FAKE NEWS!

The Independent

Donald Trump admits US taxpayer will fund his border wall... but claims Mexico will repay costs

President-elect will reportedly seek funding as soon as April for the estimated $14 billion (£11 billion) project [109]

---

109 http://www.independent.co.uk/news/world/americas/us-elections/
donald-trump-us-congress-funding-mexico-border-wall-south-fence-illegal-
immigration-a7512426.html

@realDonaldTrump 6 Jan 2017
The dishonest media does not report that any money spent on building the Great Wall (for sake of speed), will be paid back by Mexico later!

After his inauguration, there was a significant reduction in his social media traffic but as January 2017 came to an end, Trump was back on his personal Twitter account and once again had accused the *New York Times* of spreading fake news.

@realDonaldTrump 28 Jan 2017
The failing @nytimes has been wrong about me from the very beginning. Said I would lose the primaries, then the general election. FAKE NEWS!

January: Inauguration

On January 20, 2017, Donald Trump became President Trump, 45th President of the United States. The inauguration was a massive multi-day event on the American calendar as thousands of people streamed into the nation's capital to witness and celebrate democracy in motion.

@realDonaldTrump 19 Jan 2017
the American people. I have no doubt that we will, together, MAKE AMERICA GREAT AGAIN!

The night before his inauguration, Trump held the 'Make America Great Again' inauguration concert at the Lincoln memorial. Performers included 3 Doors Down, The Piano Guys and country singer Toby Keith. Trump's concert had an estimated turnout of 10,000 people.

@realDonaldTrump 19 Jan 2017
Thank you for joining us at the Lincoln Memorial tonight- a very special evening! Together, we are going to MAKE AMERICA GREAT AGAIN!

By comparison, Obama's concert in 2009 had an estimated 400,000 people in attendance and included performances from the likes of Bon Jovi, U2 and Bruce Springsteen.

Although Trump dominated social media for the best part of 18 months, the reduced physical turn out of people provided an interesting contrast.[110]

---

110 http://www.independent.co.uk/news/world/americas/donald-trump-inaugural-concert-crowds-looked-smaller-than-barack-obamas-a7536531.html

To tweet or not to tweet

After observing Trump's Twitter behaviour, it was disappointing to note that he did not (either himself or via his team) live tweet through the inauguration, in fact in the days leading up to the inauguration, Trump went very quiet on social media, tweeting less than 10 times a day.

@realDonaldTrump 20 Jan 2017
It all begins today! I will see you at 11:00 A.M. for the swearing-in. THE MOVEMENT CONTINUES – THE WORK BEGINS!

Hillary Clinton tweeted her presence at the inauguration:

@HillaryClinton 20 Jan 2017
I'm here today to honour our democracy & its enduring values. I will never stop believing in our country & its future. #Inauguration

The hashtags #InaugurationDay and #ThanksObamas were trending on Twitter with tweets coming into the @POTUS twitter accounts thanking him for his eight years in office and threatening to unfollow once Trump took over.

The world watched as Trump became President. At the point when the @POTUS account switched from Barack Obama to Donald Trump, the followers dropped from 13 million to 3 million. This dip however was only temporary, within a few hours Trump surpassed the previous POTUS's numbers.

Presidential tweets

After a few hours of zero social media activity on the @POTUS or @realDonaldTrump accounts (I guess he was a little busy) Trump tweeted his first tweet as POTUS:

President Trump @POTUS 21 Jan 2017
On behalf of my entire family, THANK YOU! #InaugurationDay 🦅 .

Presidential? Yes, and appropriate, but after having tracked his social media habits, I expected something bolder from Trump.

Maybe his old Twitter account would deliver.

@realDonaldTrump 21 Jan 2017
Today we are not merely transferring power from one Administration to another, or from one party to another – but we are transferring...

@realDonaldTrump 21 Jan 2017
power from Washington, D.C. and giving it back to you, the American People. #InaugurationDay

@realDonaldTrump 21 Jan 2017
What truly matters is not which party controls our government, but whether our government is controlled by the people.

@realDonaldTrump 21 Jan 2017
January 20th 2017, will be remembered as the day the people became the rulers of this nation again.

@realDonaldTrump 21 Jan 2017
The forgotten men and women of our country will be forgotten no longer. From this moment on, it's going to be #AmericaFirst 🇺🇸

@realDonaldTrump 21 Jan 2017
We will bring back our jobs. We will bring back our borders. We will bring back our wealth - and we will bring back our dreams!

@realDonaldTrump 21 Jan 2017
We will follow two simple rules: BUY AMERICAN & HIRE AMERICAN! #InaugurationDay 🦅 #MAGA 🇺🇸

Apparently bored of breaking the speech up into 146 character chunks, Trump moved to Facebook:

Donald J. Trump
Facebook
January 21, 2017

It is time to remember that old wisdom our soldiers will never forget: that whether we are black or brown or white, we all bleed the same red blood of patriots!

So to all Americans, in every city near and far, small and large, from mountain to mountain, and from ocean to ocean, hear these words:

You will never be ignored again!

To Americans: You will never be ignored again. Your voice, your hopes and your dreams will define our American destiny. Your courage and goodness and love will forever guide us along the way.

Together we will make America strong again. We will make
America wealthy again. We will make America proud again.
We will make America safe again - and yes, together,
WE WILL MAKE AMERICA GREAT AGAIN![111]

What you have just read are the 'highlights' of his 16-minute
inauguration speech.

Peaceful protest

On the day of Trump's inauguration, feminist groups all
over the US and around the world protested against
President Trump.

@France4Hillary 21 Jan 2017

#WomensMarch:

LA: 750,000

DC: 500,000

NYC: 250,000

Chicago: 250,000

Boston: 125,000

AND MILLIONS ALL OVER THE WORLD!!

@jazzzhand 21 Jan 2017
I heard there were zero arrests today at the
#WomensMarch **DC. It's time for women to**
run our country. Violence and hate are over.

---

111 https://www.facebook.com/DonaldTrump

> **@zacksabrejr** 21 Jan 2017
> **Congratulations to everyone who peacefully protested at #womensmarch around the world today.**
> **Big up London.**

> **@Rooting4OBAMA** 22 Jan 2017
> **This Women March in Australia is HUGE.**
> #WomensMarch #Melbourne #ProtestTrump
> #TheResistance #NotMyPresident

Presidential controversy

The whitehouse.gov website fully transitioned to reflect the new administration. As the site updated to reflect the policies of President Trump, people were shocked to see a number of pages disappear.

People understand that the purpose of whitehouse.gov is to reflect the policies of the current administration, but there was a general sense of fear regarding people's freedom, since a large proportion of Trump's policies point towards an America which is closed off to the world. Given Trump's harassment of the media, and the media's rabid hunger to report anything controversial from the Trump camp, the media reported on the changes to the whitehouse.gov site with some sensational headlines.

The Independent

Donald Trump inauguration: US civil rights history deleted from White House website under new President[112]

CBS News

Moments after Donald Trump became president, the White House's LGBT rights page disappeared[113]

Esquire

Civil Rights, Climate Change, and Healthcare Were All Scrubbed from the White House Website[114]

Climate change   whitehouse.gov/energy/climate-change

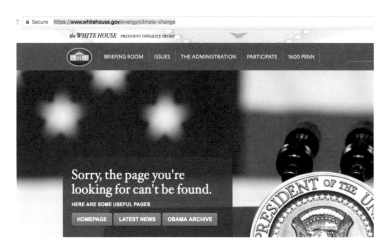

---

112   http://www.independent.co.uk/news/world/americas/donald-trump-inauguration-civil-rights-deleted-white-house-website-a7538581.html

113   http://www.cbsnews.com/news/moments-after-donald-trump-became-president-the-white-houses-lgbt-rights-page-disappeared/

114   http://www.esquire.com/news-politics/news/a52430/white-house-website-changes

Civil rights history whitehouse.gov/issues/civil-rights

LGBT whitehouse.gov/lgbt

Healthcare   whitehouse.gov/the-record/health-care

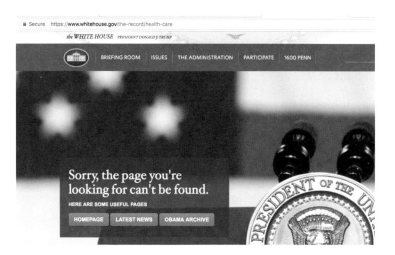

Upon employing the 'search' function on the whitehouse.org website, 'LGBT' brings up zero results. The other terms link to obscure documents about the health of former first ladies, historical documents about the American Civil War and a search for 'climate change' produces one result:

> Mamie Geneva Doud Eisenhower
> Married at the age of 19, Mamie Geneva Doud Eisenhower was the wife of the 34th President, Dwight D. Eisenhower, and a very popular First Lady of the United States from 1953 to 1961.[115]

If you know the exact URL you are trying to reach, such as "www.whitehouse.gov/LGBT" you are taken to the '404 error page not found' page which does have a link to the 'ObamaArchive', an archived version of the 44th President's whitehouse.gov pages. The pages are available but one needs to take a very convoluted route to get there and there does not appear to be a direct link from the new whitehouse.gov landing page.

---

115   https://www.whitehouse.gov/1600/first-ladies/mamieeisenhower

A person could argue that there does not need to be a link back to the 'old guard', but with such a controversial election and candidate and with uncertainty over immigration and healthcare, it seems short-sighted of the website administrators as it proved to feed the fear of Trump and his policies.

Celebrities, such as George Takei tweeted:

> **@GeorgeTakei** 20 Jan 2017
> **The White House removed its climate change web page. And the healthcare, civil rights and LGBT sections. Just thought you should know.**

LGBT and US Civil rights history was an integral part of Obama's administration not only because he broke ground by becoming the first black President but the cultural significance of his inauguration indicated a bright future of equality for everyone in the US.

On January 31, 2017, President Trump released a statement acknowledging that he was proud to be the first GOP nominee to mention the LGBT community in his inauguration speech and that he would continue to enact the executive order signed in 2014 which protects the LGBT community in the workplace.[116]

The only plan not present on the new White House website is a healthcare plan. Trump has repeatedly stated that he will repeal and replace the Affordable Care Act (ACA) as a priority:

> @realDonaldTrump 12 Jan 2017
> **Congrats to the Senate for taking the first step to #RepealObamacare - now it's onto the House!**

---

116 https://www.whitehouse.gov/the-press-office/2017/01/31/president-donald-j-trump-will-continue-enforce-executive-order

Whitehouse.gov reflects the polices of the current administration. The sensationalist reporting on the new site by the press plays on the fears of the left-leaning section of the US who read the removal of pages relating to civil rights, healthcare, LGBT and climate change as a sign of dark times ahead but the site is simply reflecting the main policies of the new President.

It is clear what is not on the new White House site, so one should look at what *is* there:

Energy — *An America First Energy Plan*

The Trump Administration is also committed to clean coal technology, and to reviving America's coal industry, which has been hurting for too long.

In addition to being good for our economy, boosting domestic energy production is in America's national security interest. President Trump is committed to achieving energy independence from the OPEC cartel and any nations hostile to our interests. At the same time, we will work with our Gulf allies to develop a positive energy relationship as part of our anti-terrorism strategy.

Lastly, our need for energy must go hand-in-hand with responsible stewardship of the environment. Protecting clean air and clean water, conserving our natural habitats, and preserving our natural reserves and resources will remain a high priority. President Trump will refocus the EPA on its essential mission of protecting our air and water.[117]

Foreign Policy: Peace through strength & US-centric Trade deals — *America First Foreign Policy*

We will rebuild the American military. Our Navy has shrunk from more than 500 ships in 1991 to 275 in 2016. Our Air Force is roughly one third smaller than in 1991. President Trump is committed to reversing this trend, because he knows that our military dominance must be unquestioned.

---

117   https://www.whitehouse.gov/america-first-energy

Withdrawing from the Trans-Pacific Partnership and making certain that any new trade deals are in the interests of American workers. President Trump is committed to renegotiating NAFTA. If our partners refuse a renegotiation that gives American workers a fair deal, then the President will give notice of the United States' intent to withdraw from NAFTA.[118]

Jobs — *Bringing Back Jobs And Growth*

To get the economy back on track, President Trump has outlined a bold plan to create 25 million new American jobs in the next decade and return to 4 percent annual economic growth.[119]

Big Guns — *Making Our Military Strong Again*

Our military needs every asset at its disposal to defend America. We cannot allow other nations to surpass our military capability. The Trump Administration will pursue the highest level of military readiness.[120]

New Sheriff(s) — *Standing Up For Our Law Enforcement Community*

Supporting law enforcement means supporting our citizens' ability to protect themselves. We will uphold Americans' Second Amendment rights at every level of our judicial system.

President Trump is committed to building a border wall to stop illegal immigration, to stop the gangs and the violence, and to stop the drugs from pouring into our communities.[121]

National Parks punishment

A late breaking story on the day of the inauguration, originally published by gizmodo.com and later picked up by the mainstream media, is a tale which hints at the idea of State censorship:

---

118   https://www.whitehouse.gov/america-first-foreign-policy

119   https://www.whitehouse.gov/bringing-back-jobs-and-growth

120   https://www.whitehouse.gov/making-our-military-strong-again

121   https://www.whitehouse.gov/making-our-military-strong-again

gizmodo.com

National Park Service Banned From Tweeting After Anti-Trump Retweets

The National Park service retweeted some sick Donald Trump burns, noting how, uh, lightly attended his inauguration was compared to Barack Obama's in 2009. But now, the NPS has been ordered by its Washington support office to "immediately cease use of government Twitter accounts until further notice," according to an internal email obtained by Gizmodo.[122]

The National Parks Service took down the 'offending' post. Gizmodo published a copy of the letter sent to the National Park Service.

> **All:**
>
> We have received direction from the Department through [the Washington Support Office] that directs all [Department of Interior] bureaus to immediately cease use of government Twitter accounts until further notice.
>
> PWR parks that use Twitter as part of their crisis communications plans need to alter their contingency plans to accommodate this requirement. Please ensure all scheduled posts are deleted and automated cross-platform social media connections to your twitter accounts are severed. The expectation is that there will be absolutely no posts to Twitter.
>
> In summary, this Twitter stand down means we will cease use of Twitter immediately. However, there is no need to suspend or delete government accounts until directed.
>
> This does not affect use of other approved social media platforms. We expect further guidance to come next week and we will share accordingly.
>
> Thanks for your help![123]

---

122 http://gizmodo.com/national-park-service-banned-from-tweeting-after-anti-t-1791449526

123 http://gizmodo.com/national-park-service-banned-from-tweeting-after-anti-t-1791449526

The Independent

US Interior Department ordered to 'immediately cease' use of official Twitter accounts after anti-Trump retweets

Ban comes after National Park Service Twitter account retweets images comparing the people that turned out for Mr Obama's inauguration with the smaller crowds for Mr Trump.[124]

The 'ban' is of concern because it appeared to be in reaction to an embarrassing photograph comparing crowd sizes between Trump's 2017 inauguration and Obama's 2009 inauguration.

---

124 http://www.independent.co.uk/news/world/americas/donald-trump-interior-department-twitter-retweets-ordered-shut-down-a7538951.html

The next day, the National Parks Service is able to tweet again, they posted:

@NatlParkService Jan 21 2017
We regret the mistaken RTs from our account yesterday and look forward to continuing to share the beauty and history of our parks with you

The only 'official' comment from President Trump or the White House on media coverage is this tweet:

@realDonaldTrump 22 Jan 2017
Wow, television ratings just out: 31 million people watched the Inauguration, 11 million more than the very good ratings from 4 years ago!

Responses to Trump's tweet sparked further controversy when there were accusations from one Twitter user that team Trump are editing the Twitter comments stream and 'disconnecting' comments which counter the message Trump is communicating.

@AJ More 22 Jan 2017
@realDonaldTrump **wait what? This includes live streaming which has only been established in recent times...also maybe watching in disbelief**

At the request of other users, @AJ_More posts a screenshot which demonstrates that the Trump twitter team 'edited out' his comment:

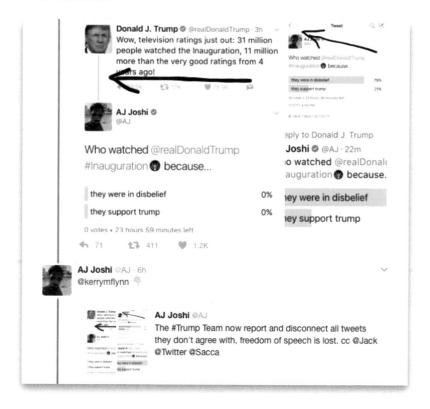

Whether this was an example of State censorship or the @realDonaldTrump administration simply reporting and removing posts that they considered 'trolling' is worth keeping an eye on.

Looking ahead

'I find it tremendous. It's a modern form of communication. There should be nothing we should be ashamed of....I think that social media has more power than the money they [Democrats] spent, and I think maybe to a certain extent, I proved that.'[125]

It is hard to imagine what the 2016 US election would have looked like, or how it would have turned out, if Donald Trump had not been a savvy social media operator. Following his election victory, Trump spoke about his implementation of social media with CBS:

'When you give me a bad story or when you give me an inaccurate story or when somebody other than you and another— a network, or whatever, because of course, CBS would never do a thing like that right? I have a method of fighting back.'[126]

Whenever a bad news story was published about Trump and his campaign, Trump tweeted his protest, accusing a variety of media outlets of bias and the producers of fake news. The question to ask is, did Trump use his reach of tens of millions of twitter followers to set the record straight, to add balance to a media machine that is bias towards the old ways of Government or did he, under the premise of balance, use it to add additional spin to his digital campaign? In the multi-faceted age of information there is never only one reported side to a story, with 24-hour news coverage and a variety of blogging and social media platforms giving the general public an opportunity to tell a story 'in the moment', the digestion of news has become an increasingly subjective experience, so only you, reader, can answer that question.

---

125 CBS 60 minutes preview, November 13, 2016, cbsnews.com

126 http://www.politico.com/story/2016/11/donald-trump-social-media-231285

The way that people think a democracy works is that the person or party that can convince the most people to back them is the winner, the reality is slightly different – as the popular vote versus the electoral college vote numbers indicate – but for the sake of simplicity, the basic idea is still largely true.

Regardless, due to the developments in broadcasting technology and the digital landscape, government is no longer a faceless system. Western governments now have to run their campaigns like popularity contests and the people who head those governments need to be savvy operators of 'the new technology' if they ever hope to connect with the common person.

Trump deciding to use social media or a new form of media during his campaign isn't exactly new; politicians have been using social media for a number of years to communicate ideas to voters. At the beginning of the 20th century Theodore Roosevelt sent the first transatlantic telegraph from the United States to the United Kingdom, and in 1955 John F. Kennedy was the first US President to fully recognise and embrace television as a medium for communicating with 'the people'.

Trump treated the election as a marketing campaign for the POTUS 45 brand and used social media as the megaphone-wielding advertising and promotions manager — that part was groundbreaking. Trump not only got people talking about POTUS 45 but he got people talking about Trump as POTUS 45.

Were some of the things that Trump said during his campaign inappropriate? Quite probably, let's face it, if he had not tweeted to the extent and as brashly as he did, I wouldn't be writing a book about him. The morality of his campaign is not in question here, the entire nation, even if they all did not vote, were engaged in a political discussion – even if it was simply a discussion over the legitimacy of Trump as a candidate for the Presidency.

How he did it is simple. If he had an opinion, he expressed it and often without the etiquette that one expects from a person of his influence. That is what attracted the voters, his apparent lack of political bullshitting, his apparent lack of political spin. Although as the narratives I have explored in this book suggest, almost every tweet had an agenda behind it.

There was some talk that Trump's campaign had only been a popularity contest, that some of his promises were on the level of a high school council election, that he was promising to give all his voters free pizza on Friday if they voted for him. But within hours of his inauguration he began to follow through with the promises he made.

Between the inauguration and February 1, 2017, a mere eleven days into his four years he signed the following executive orders:

January 20

'Executive order minimizing the economic burden of the Patient Protection and Affordable Care Act, pending repeal.'

Trump gave State Senators the power to relax and even blatantly ignore the laws put into place under ObamaCare in what has to be seen as a way of easing state budgets away from ObamaCare and into the new healthcare system, when one is created.

January 24

'Expediting environmental reviews and approvals for high priority infrastructure projects.'

Trump is sticking true to his "jobs" policy and easing the legislation so that he can build roads to decrease unemployment by literally building roads and laying down legislation for the express approval of the Keystone XL oil pipeline.

January 25

'Enhancing public safety in the interior of the United States.'

Phase one of Trump's big immigration crackdown.
The legislation indicates that Sanctuary cities are to be no more and Trump reminded the immigration enforcement agency that they are to use the full force of the law when dealing with illegal aliens.

'Border security and immigration enforcement improvements.'

This is the big one, Trump *is* going to build a wall along the southern border, he's also going to build a big prison to put people who are caught trying to cross the border illegally.

January 27

'Protecting the nation from foreign terrorist entry into the United States.'

January 28

'Ethics commitments by executive branch appointees.'

This is Trump's #DrainTheSwamp policy to restrict executive branch employees from lobbying for the US government or a foreign government during the first five years after they leave their job, part of his plan to eliminate the nepotism and 'old-boy network' within the US.

January 30

'Reducing regulation and controlling regulatory costs.'

'For fiscal year 2017, which is in progress, the heads of all agencies are directed that the total incremental cost of all new regulations, including repealed regulations, to be finalized this year shall be no greater than zero, unless otherwise required by law or consistent with advice provided in writing by the Director of the Office of Management and Budget (Director).'

Trump is freezing government budgets.

After one of the most interesting and, possibly, most widely covered US election campaigns. A former head of a company with global reach, with no political experience, is now the head of a country with significant global reach, and he is still tweeting.

A letter to the reader

Trump is the product of a society driven by the media, of a culture of popularity. A book about Trump tweeting only truly finishes when Trump stops tweeting. If I took that approach, I would still be editing this book now. Instead I looked for natural breaks such as Inauguration Day – the moment the candidate became the leader – which is why this book only goes as far as the end of January 2017.

As Trump pursues the risqué policies he campaigned for, as his advisors are appointed or resign, I am watching and taking note. There will be more books as Trump's political milestones become my editorial deadlines.

This book would not have been possible without the help of the designers Matt and Dan, my editor Jess and the many others who helped me refine my words and sharpen the design to present this book.

I would also like to acknowledge the website trumpthetwitterarchive.com whose meticulous archiving of almost every Trump tweet made the search for narrative that little bit easier.

James and the team behind Trump Tweets
trumptweetsbooks.com